Editor Project Manager
Mara Ellen Guckian

Illustrator
Kelly McMahon

Cover Artist
Marilyn Goldberg

Managing Editor
Ina Massler Levin, M.A.

Creative Director
Karen J. Goldfluss, M.S. Ed.

Art Production Manager
Kevin Barnes

Art Coordinator
Renée Christine Yates

Imaging
Nathan P. Rivera

Publisher
Mary D. Smith, M.S. Ed.

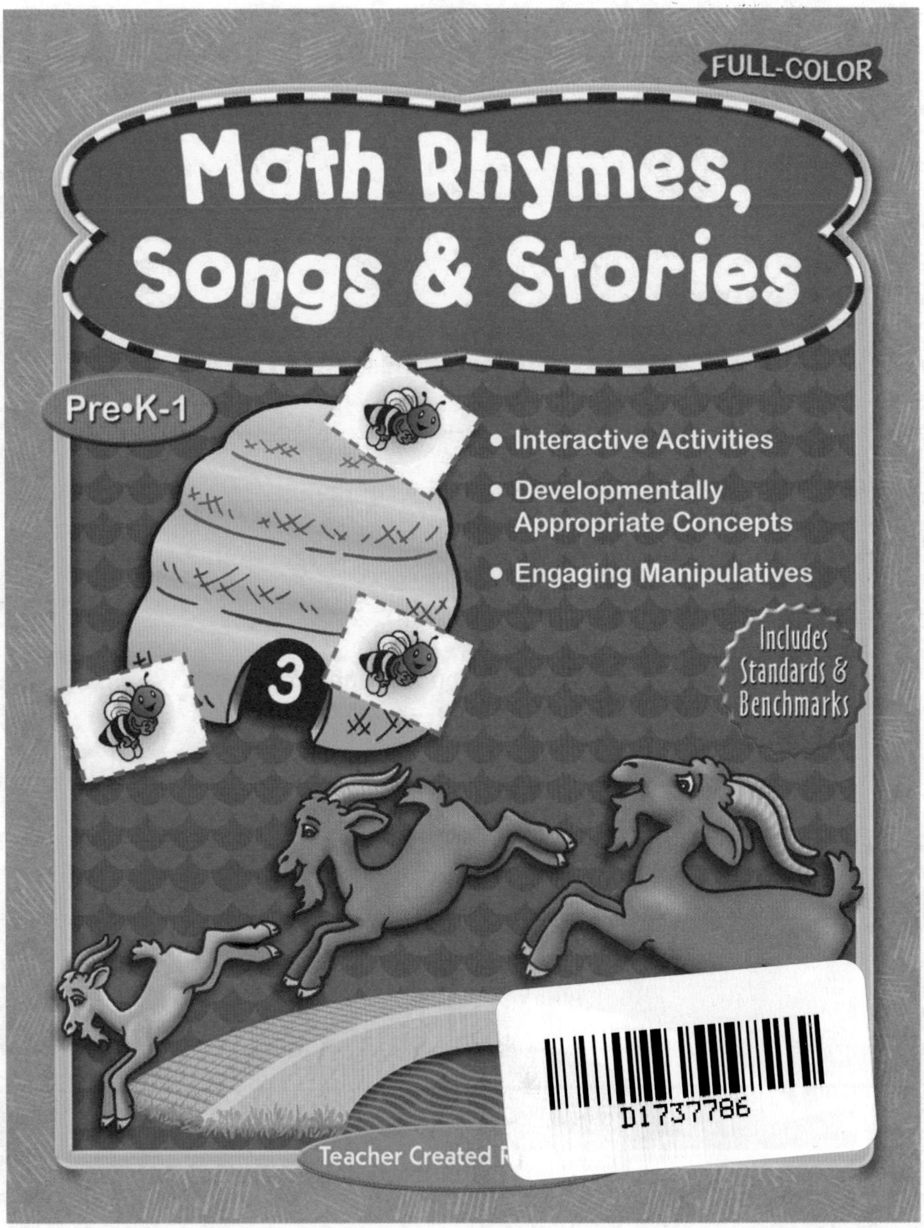

FULL-COLOR

Math Rhymes, Songs & Stories

Pre•K-1

- Interactive Activities
- Developmentally Appropriate Concepts
- Engaging Manipulatives

Includes Standards & Benchmarks

3

D1737786

Teacher Created R

Author

Tracy Edmunds, M.S. Ed.

Teacher Created Resources, Inc.
6421 Industry Way
Westminster, CA 92683
www.teachercreated.com
ISBN: 978-1-4206-8857-3

Made in U.S.A.

Table of Contents

Introduction

Math can be fun! *Math Rhymes, Songs, and Stories* helps Pre-K, Kindergarten, and first grade teachers engage students' interest with full-color teaching tools that make math fun and exciting. Each unit includes activities that can be used to introduce, practice, or reinforce developmentally appropriate math concepts. All lessons are tied directly to the national McREL math standards, as listed on the *Activities* pages of each unit.

Rhyme, Song, and Story Mini Posters

Each colorfully illustrated rhyme, song, or story mini poster comes ready to laminate and display in the classroom. On the back of each color mini poster is a black and white version to copy for students. They can read along, color the illustrations, and take their mini posters home to share with their families.

Puppets

The full-color puppet patterns can be used to retell the rhymes, songs, and stories and to practice math concepts with students. Simply cut them out, laminate them, and attach them to craft sticks or straws. Several units also include reproducible puppets that students can color, cut out, and use on their own.

Counters and Cut Outs

Several of the units include full-color counters and manipulatives to cut out, laminate, and use with students. See the *Activities* page of each unit for instructions on using these manipulatives with students for hands-on practice and reinforcement of math concepts.

Mini Books

Reproducible, easy-to-assemble mini books are included for two rhymes and two stories. Copy the *Goldilocks and the Three Bears* and *Three Billy Goats Gruff* mini books for students and let them color the illustrations and read the books to each other or to family members. The mini books for *Five Green Frogs* and *Five Little Monkeys* are interactive and allow students to practice addition and subtraction concepts.

Numeral, Operation Symbol, and Number Word Cards

The *Numeral, Operation Symbol*, and *Number Word Cards* at the beginning of the Number Sense unit can be cut out and laminated for use in pocket charts during whole-class or small-group instruction. The *Days of the Week* and *Months of the Year Word Cards* can be copied, cut out, and laminated for use with the Calendar unit. The *Shape Word Cards* can be cut out and laminated for use with the Shapes unit. See the *Activities* section of each unit for suggested uses of these teaching tools.

Reproducible Pages

Most of the units include reproducible worksheets for student practice. All worksheets are tied directly to the standards addressed in the units so they can also be used as assessment tools.

Standards

Standard 1: Uses a variety of strategies in the problem-solving process

K-2

- Draws pictures to represent problems
- Uses discussions with teachers and other students to understand problems
- Uses whole number models (e.g., pattern blocks, tiles, or other manipulative materials) to represent problems

Standard 2: Understands and applies basic and advanced properties of the concepts of numbers

Pre-K

- Understands that numbers represent the quantity of objects
- Counts by ones to ten or higher
- Counts objects
- Understands one-to-one correspondence
- Understands the concept of position in a sequence (e.g., first, last)
- Knows the written numerals 0-9
- Knows the common language for comparing quantity of objects (e.g., "more than," "less than," "same as")

K-2

- Understands that numerals are symbols used to represent quantities or attributes of real-world objects
- Counts whole numbers (i.e., both cardinal and ordinal numbers)
- Understands symbolic, concrete, and pictorial representations of numbers (e.g., written numerals, objects in sets, number lines)
- Understands basic whole number relationships (e.g., 4 is less than 10, 30 is 3 tens)

Standard 3: Uses basic and advanced procedures while performing the processes of computation

Pre-K

- Knows that the quantity of objects can change by adding or taking away objects

K-2

- Adds and subtracts whole numbers
- Solves real-world problems involving addition and subtraction of whole numbers
- Understands the inverse relationship between addition and subtraction

Standards *(cont.)*

Standard 4: Understands and applies basic and advanced properties of the concepts of measurement

Pre-K

- Orders objects qualitatively by measurable attribute (e.g., smallest to largest, lightest to heaviest, shortest to longest)
- Knows the common language of measurement (e.g., "big," "little," "long," "short," "light," "heavy")

Standard 5: Understands and applies basic and advanced properties of the concepts of geometry

Pre-K

- Knows basic geometric language for naming shapes (e.g., circle, triangle, square, rectangle)
- Understands the common language used to describe position and location (e.g., "up," "down," "below," "above," "beside," "inside," "outside")

K-2

- Understands basic properties of (e.g., number of sides, corners, square corners) and similarities and differences between simple geometric shapes
- Understands the common language of spatial sense (e.g., "left," "right," "horizontal," "in front of")

Standard 8: Understands and applies basic and advanced properties of functions and algebra

Pre-K

- Understands simple patterns (e.g., boy-girl-boy-girl)
- Repeats simple patterns
- Extends simple patterns (e.g., of numbers, physical objects, geometric shapes)

Kendall, J. S., & Marzano, R. J. (2004). Content knowledge: A compendium of standards and benchmarks for K-12 education. Aurora, CO: Mid-continent Research for Education and Learning. Online database: http://www.mcrel.org/standards-benchmarks/

Number Sense

Pre-K and Kindergarten students are often just beginning to form a sense of what numbers are and how they work. Number sense is the vital foundation on which students will build much of their future mathematical knowledge. Many first graders have not solidified number sense. They too benefit from additional hands-on practice. It is important that they internalize these concepts and practice them often.

Most students first learn to count by *rote*, just saying the number names in order. While this is a necessary skill, it is important that their learning not stop there! When children learn to say counting words in order, they often do not know how to count one item for each number. For example, if you give Sarah five blocks and ask her to count them, she may say, "One, two, three, four, five, six, seven," while randomly pointing to the blocks. Sarah has not yet grasped *one-to-one correspondence*—matching one number to one item when counting. Students need to practice this concept in concrete form, doing hands-on exercises with real objects. The counters, puppets, and manipulatives in this unit are great tools for helping students practice one-to-one correspondence.

Once children can count with one-to-one correspondence, they need many experiences with quantities and numerals to form a basic understanding of numbers that they can build on throughout their lives. They need to practice comparing sets of objects using "more than," "less than," and "equal." They need to understand what happens when you take some objects away from a set, what happens when you add more objects, and how those actions can be written using numbers and symbols. They need to understand the relationships between addition and subtraction and how they work together. Young children need to use real objects, models, and pictures to practice these basic concepts.

The rhymes, songs, tools, and activities in this unit are perfect for introducing and practicing these important number sense concepts with young students. The following standards and benchmarks can be taught using the tools and activities in this unit:

- *Counts whole numbers (i.e., both cardinal and ordinal numbers)*
- *Counts by ones to ten or higher*
- *Knows the written numerals 0-9*
- *Understands that numbers represent the quantity of objects*
- *Understands one-to-one correspondence*
- *Knows that the quantity of objects in a group can change by adding more objects*
- *Knows that the quantity of objects in a group can change by taking away some objects*
- *Knows the common language for comparing quantity of objects (e.g., "more than," "less than," "same as")*
- *Understands basic whole number relationships (e.g., 4 is less than 10)*
- *Uses whole number models to represent problems*
- *Draws pictures to represent problems*

Numeral and Operation Symbol Cards

3	7	+
2	6	10
1	5	9
0	4	8

Operation Symbol and Number Word Cards

=	two	four
−	one	three

Operation Symbol and Number Word Cards

six	eight	ten
five	seven	nine

The Beehive

Standards: Understands one-to-one correspondence, Counts 1–5

 Read "Here is the Beehive" (page 15) aloud using the following hand motions.

Here is the beehive (*show your closed fist*)
But where are the bees? (*shrug shoulders*)
Hidden away were nobody sees (*cover eyes with free hand*)
Watch and you'll see them come out of their hive (*uncover eyes*)
One, two, three, four, five (*extend fingers one at a time while counting*)
Buzzzzzzzzzz! (*Wiggle your fingers and "buzz" as the bees fly away!*)

 Have students repeat the rhyme along with you and clap for each number as they count. Then they can stomp, jump, hop, touch their toes, or high-five a neighbor while counting. Let students suggest movements to do for each number and have the class do them.

 Cut out and laminate the numeral cards (pages 7–11). Place the 1 through 5 numeral cards in a pocket chart and point to each numeral as you count the bees. Students can take turns pointing to each numeral as the class repeats the rhyme.

 On subsequent readings, have students repeat the rhyme and imitate the hand motions. Be sure to count slowly at first as students may find it difficult to extend one finger at a time.

 Cut out and laminate the numbered bee puppets and hive (pages 17 and 19). Tape craft sticks or straws to the backs to form handles. Use the bee puppets to act out the rhyme for students.

 Give the bee puppets to students and let them "fly" them back into the hive when their number is called. "Fly" each bee puppet out of the hive and "land" it on a student. Then have students line up in front of the class with their bees in the correct numerical order. The class can then count the bees aloud to check.

 Laminate and cut out the bee counters (page 21). You can make extra "bee" counters by drawing black and yellow stripes on dried beans or small rocks with markers. Make copies of the worksheet on page 14. This worksheet can be colored and laminated and used in a small group or at a center. Give each student a handful of bee counters (or other small manipulatives) andask them to put the correct number of bees on each hive.

 Once students are comfortable counting and placing the correct number of bees into each hive, give them their own copies of page 14. After they have placed the correct number of counters on each hive, have them lift off each bee and make a dot or place a small sticker underneath. When finished, they should have the correct number of bees in each hive.

 Students can practice numeral and number word recognition by matching the numbered bee puppets to the numeral and/or number word cards.

 Make copies of the poem (page 16) and have students color the bees and hive. Send the poem home with students so they can practice counting with their families.

Name: ______________________________

Counting Bees

Directions: Put the correct number of "bees" on each hive.

4

2

1

3

5

The Beehive

Here is the beehive.

But where are the bees?

Hidden away
where nobody sees.

Watch and you'll see them
come out of their hive

One, two, three, four, five

Buzzzzzzzzzzzzzz!

The Beehive

Here is the beehive.

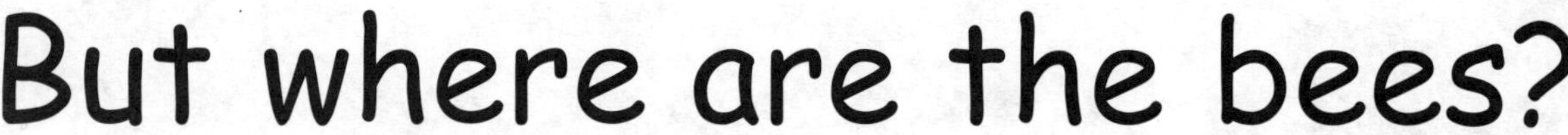

But where are the bees?

Hidden away
where nobody sees.

Watch and you'll see them
come out of their hive

One, two, three, four, five

Buzzzzzzzzzzzzz!

Bee Puppets

Bee Puppets *(cont.)*

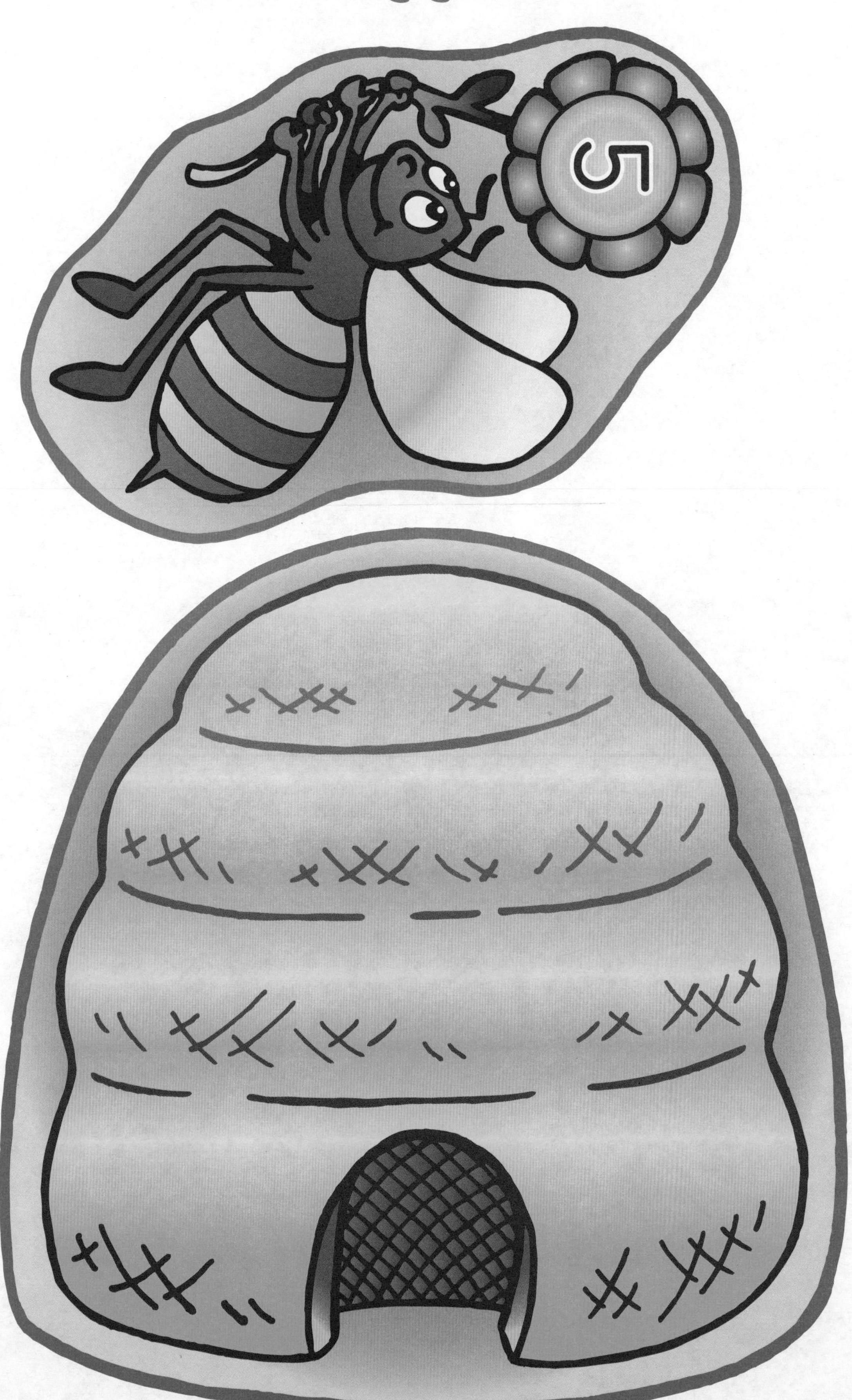

Bee Counters

There Was a Farmer

Standards: *Counts whole numbers (i.e., both cardinal and ordinal numbers)*
Counts by ones to ten or higher
Knows the written numerals 0-9

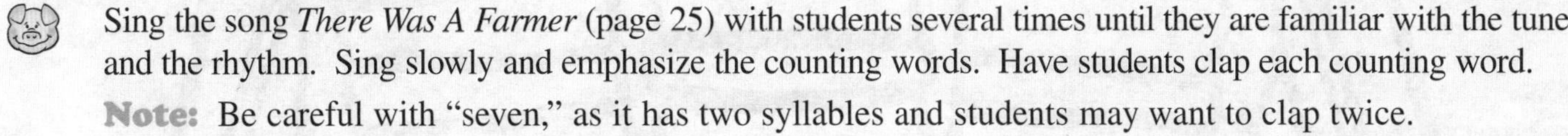

Presentation Ideas

- Sing the song *There Was A Farmer* (page 25) with students several times until they are familiar with the tune and the rhythm. Sing slowly and emphasize the counting words. Have students clap each counting word.
  Note: Be careful with "seven," as it has two syllables and students may want to clap twice.
- Have students stomp, jump, or hop for each counting word. Let students take turns leading the class in singing the song and performing the action of their choice on each counting word.
- Cut out and laminate the numbered pigs and pen (pages 27, 29, and 31). Place the 1 through 10 pigs in a pocket chart and point to each numeral as you count the animals. Students can take turns pointing to each numeral as the class repeats the rhyme.
- Place the pen in a pocket chart and give each pig to a student. Have these students line up in front of the class in number order. As you sing (slowly!), have each child put his or her pig in the pen.
- Substitute other animals and sing the song again and again. The rhythm works best with animal names that are one syllable, such as cows, ducks, chicks, and goats. If the children want to sing about animals with multi-syllable names, like horses, use the second version, leaving out "And" in the second line and "are" in the last line. Let the children suggest animals, even silly ones like elephants or dinosaurs!
- Students can use the numbered pigs to practice numeral recognition and counting.

- Give each student a handful of small manipulatives. Ask them to place the correct number on each pig.
- Set out the pigs and some clothespins or paper clips. Have students clip the correct number of clips onto each pig.
- Have students match each pig to a numeral or number word card.
- Have students close their eyes as you remove one or two pig cards and then ask them to look and identify which ones are missing.
- Make a copy of the Pig Pen worksheet (page 24) for each student. Encourage each student to draw several animals in the pen. Students can write (or dictate) the number and type of animals they added to the pen ("5 lions" or "seven bunnies") on the blank lines at the bottom. Collect the pages to make a class book and let students read it.
- Make copies of the song (page 26) and have students color the scene. Send the song home with students so they can practice counting with their families.

Name: ____________________

Pig Pen

Directions: Draw animals in the pen. Write how many animals are in the pen below.

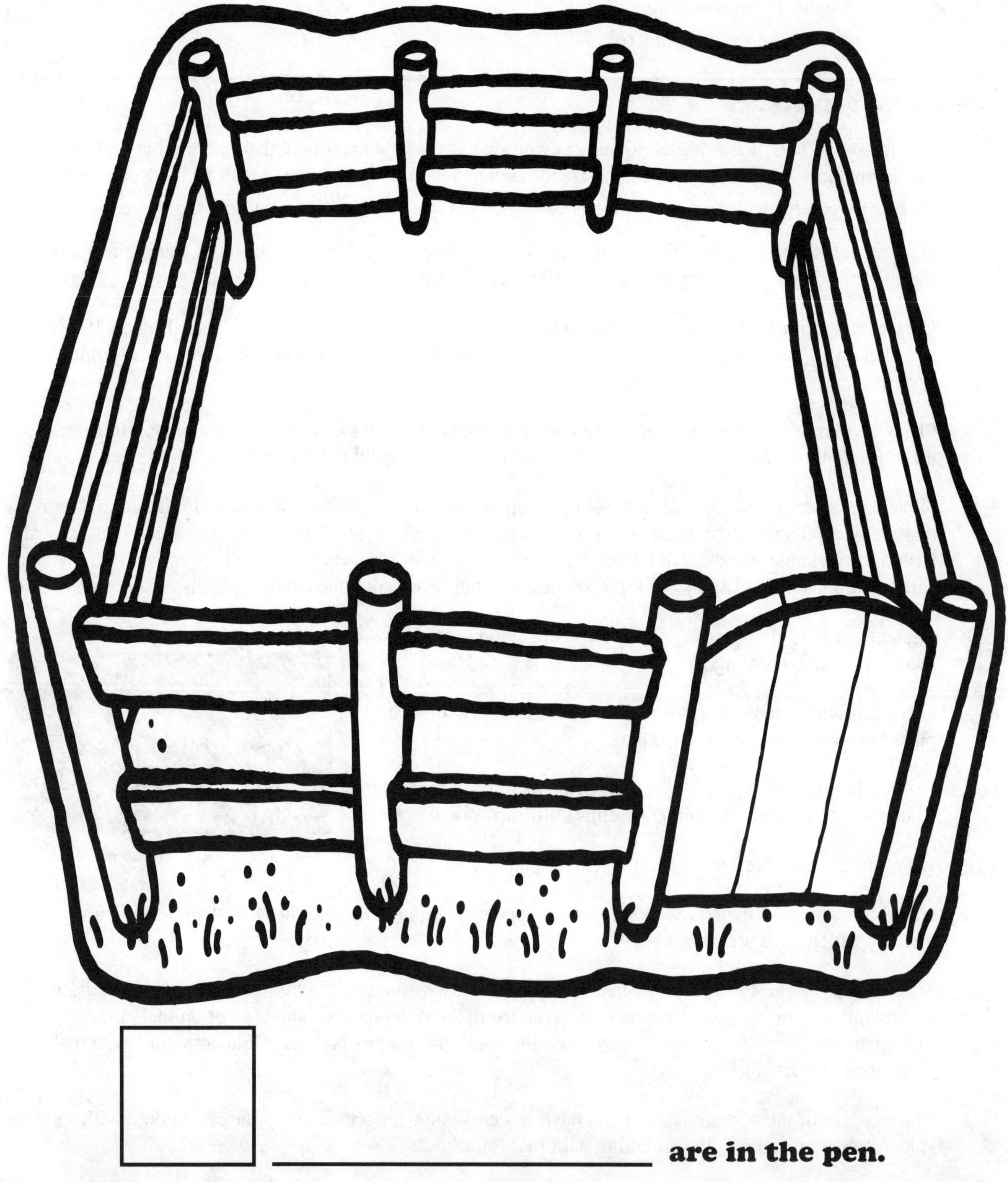

☐ ____________________ **are in the pen.**

There was a Farmer

(Sing to the tune of "Bingo.")

There was a farmer had some pigs,

And he asked me to count them.

One, two, three, four, five,

Six, seven, eight, nine, ten,

Put them in their pen.

Ten pigs are in the barnyard!

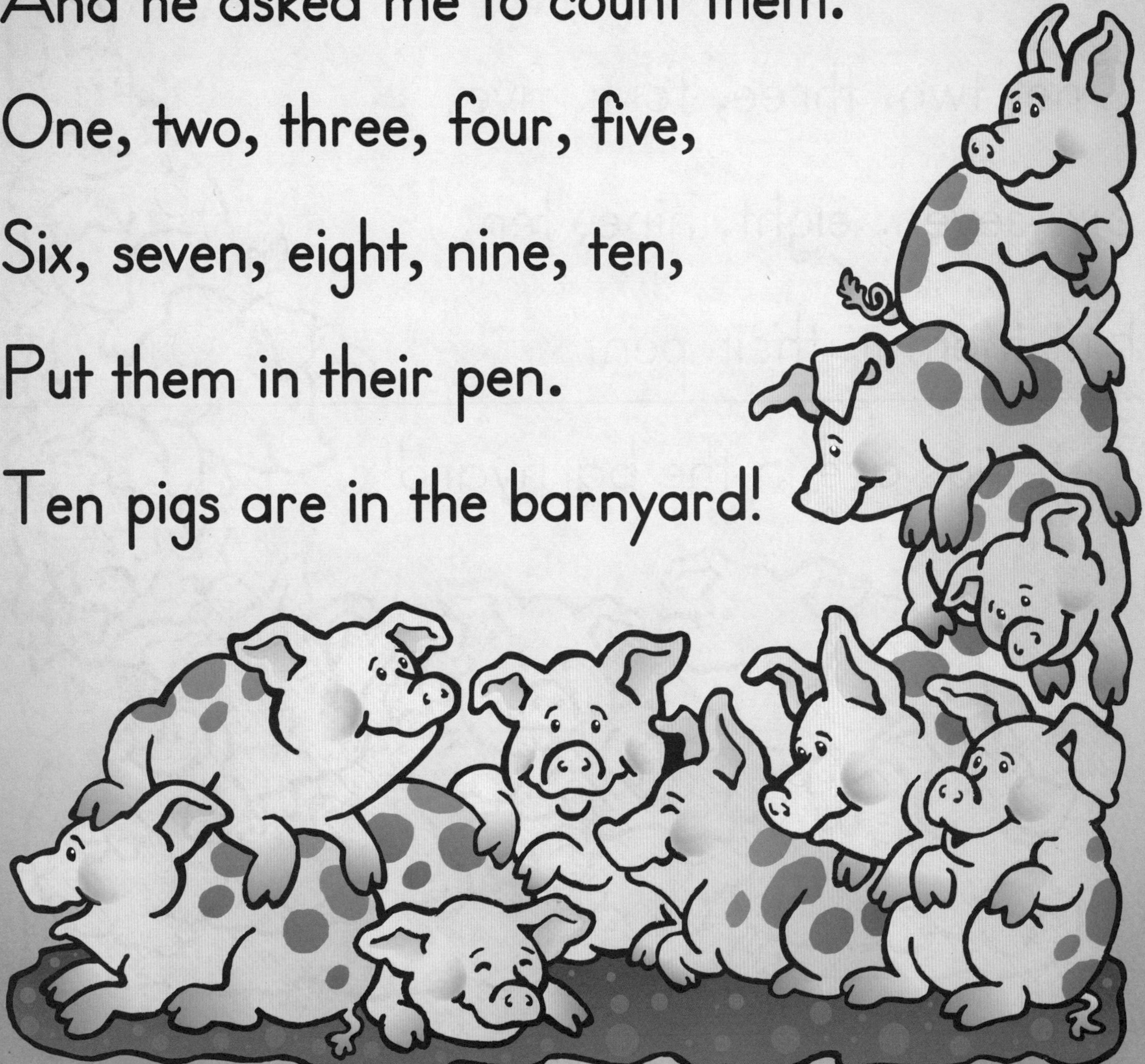

There was a Farmer

(Sing to the tune of "Bingo.")

There was a farmer had some pigs,
And he asked me to count them.
One, two, three, four, five,
Six, seven, eight, nine, ten,
Put them in their pen.
Ten pigs are in the barnyard!

Pig Puppets

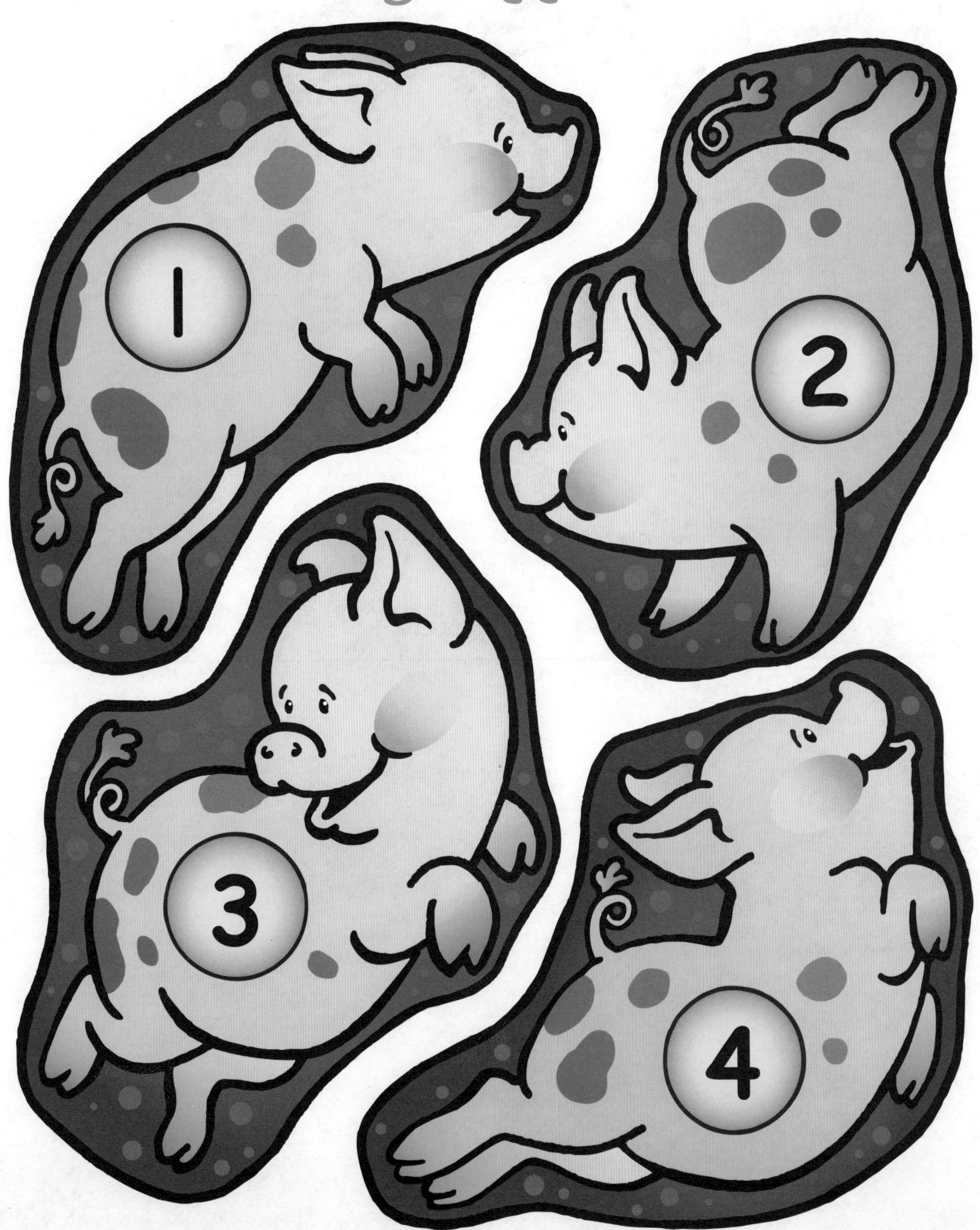

There Was A Farmer *(cont.)*

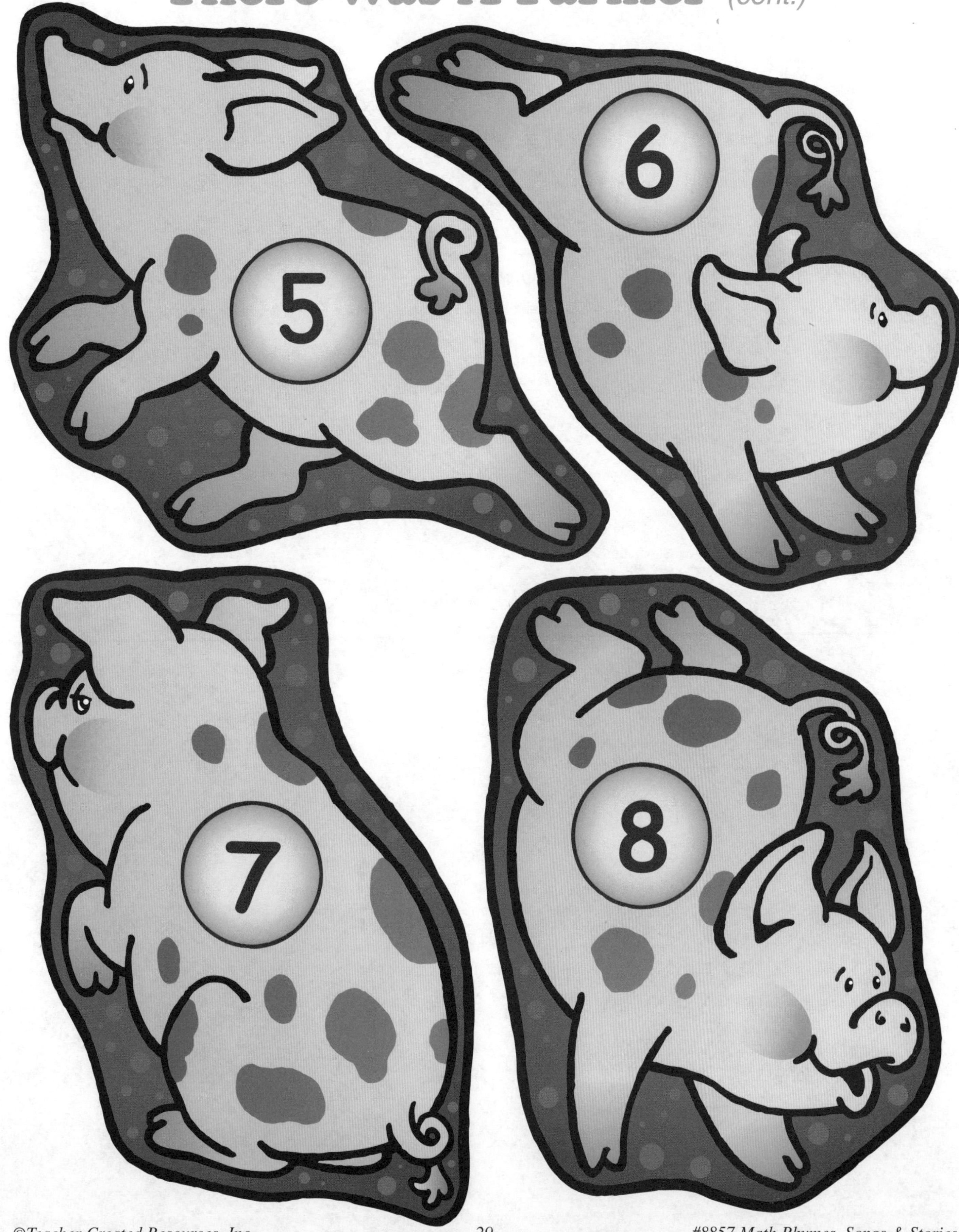

There Was A Farmer *(cont.)*

Johnny Works with One Hammer

Standards: *Understands that numbers represent the quantity of objects*
Knows that the quantity of objects in a group can change by adding more objects

Presentation Ideas

This is a building pattern song that adds one number with each verse (page 35). Sing the first verse, "Johnny works with one hammer…," ending with, "Then he works with two." Begin the next verse "Johnny works with two hammers…," and end with "Then he works with three." You can keep singing and building as long as you want!

Cut out and laminate the tool cards on pages 37 and 39. Place the hammers in a pocket chart to illustrate the song as you sing and put the appropriate numeral card (page 7) next to each hammer. For example, place one hammer and the numeral 1 in the pocket chart and sing "Johnny works with one hammer…." When you sing, "Then he works with two," add a hammer and replace the 1 numeral card with 2.

Once students are familiar with the song, replace "Johnny" with the name of a student and/or change the name of the tool, i.e., "Suzie works with eight wrenches." You can also use the number word cards (pages 9 and 11) in place of the numeral cards.

For individual hands-on practice, give the students stacking cubes and have them each build a stack to match the number of tools as you sing, adding one for each verse.

Once students are familiar with the pattern, start with a number other than one, such as, "Johnny works with four hammers…," and have students supply the end line, "Then he works with five." This is a good exercise for learning how to "count on" from a given number.

Use the color tool cards to form addition equations. Place the tools in a pocket chart to show how many are being used. For example, sing, "Tasha works with three hammers…" and place three hammers in the pocket chart with the numeral card for 3 underneath. When you get to "Then she works with four," add one tool to the pocket chart. Underneath, place the "+" symbol and the numeral card for 1, followed by the "=" symbol and the numeral card for 4. Explain to students that the "+" is a plus sign and it means "add more" and that this number sentence or equation reads, "Three plus one equals four."

You can also add more than one tool per verse. For example, tell students that Johnny will be adding two tools each time they sing a verse. Begin with "Johnny works with three hammers…" and end with, "Then he works with five." Illustrate the concept by placing the tools in the pocket chart and using the numeral and operation symbol cards to form the equation $3 + 2 = 5$.

Play "What's in the Box?" to help students practice mental addition. Have students watch you count a few tool cards and put them into a box. Then, without showing them the inside of the box, count out a few more tools and add them to the box. Ask students, "How many tools are in the box now?" After students answer, take the tools out and count them to check.

The worksheet on page 34 can be used for practice or assessment. Students count the tools in each box and write the number. Then, they draw tools in each box at the bottom to match the numeral given. If some students are not able to draw tools, let them make circles or dots.

Make copies of the rhyme (page 36) and have students color the illustrations. Send the rhyme home with students so they can practice counting with their families.

Name: ______________________________

Tool Count

Directions: Count the tools in each box and write the number below the box.

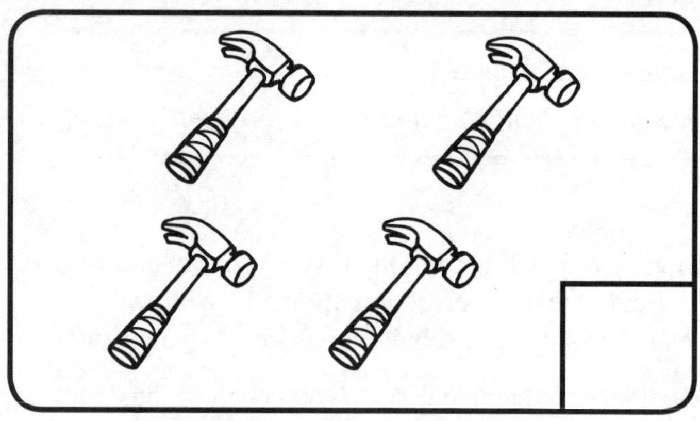

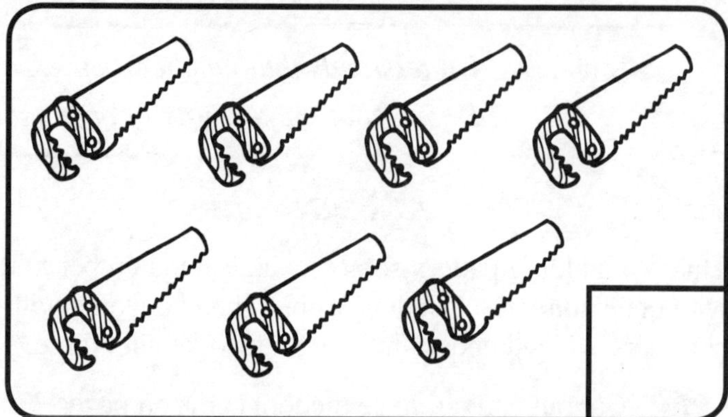

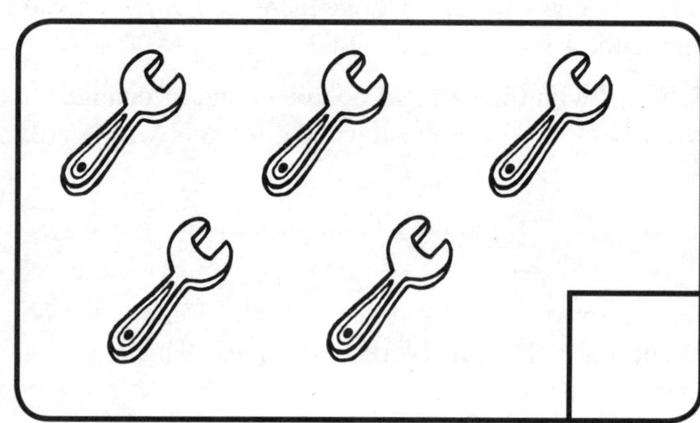

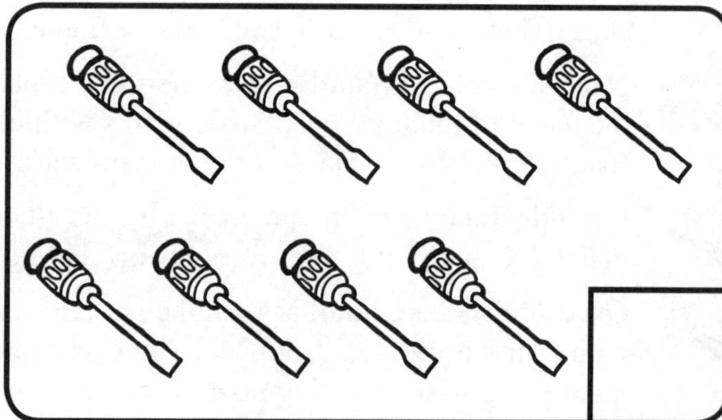

Directions: Draw the correct number of tools in each box.

Johnny Works with One Hammer

Johnny works with *one* hammer,
One hammer, *one* hammer.
Johnny works with *one* hammer,
Then he works with *two*.

Johnny works with *two* hammers,
Two hammers, *two* hammers.
Johnny works with *two* hammers,
Then he works with *three*. . .

Johnny Works with One Hammer

Johnny works with *one* hammer,
One hammer, *one* hammer.
Johnny works with *one* hammer,
Then he works with *two*.

Johnny works with *two* hammers,
Two hammers, *two* hammers.
Johnny works with *two* hammers,
Then he works with *three*. . .

Tools

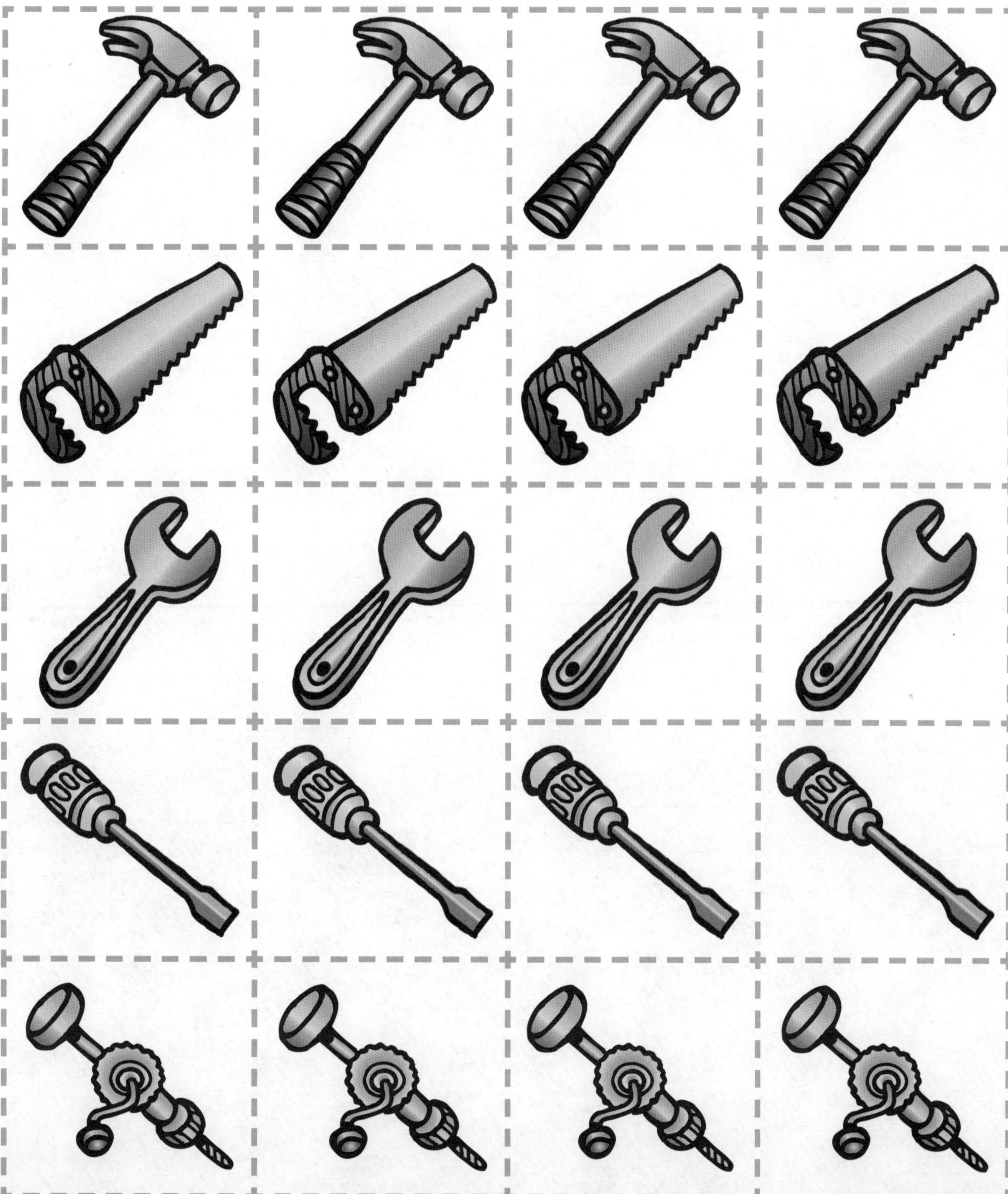

Tools

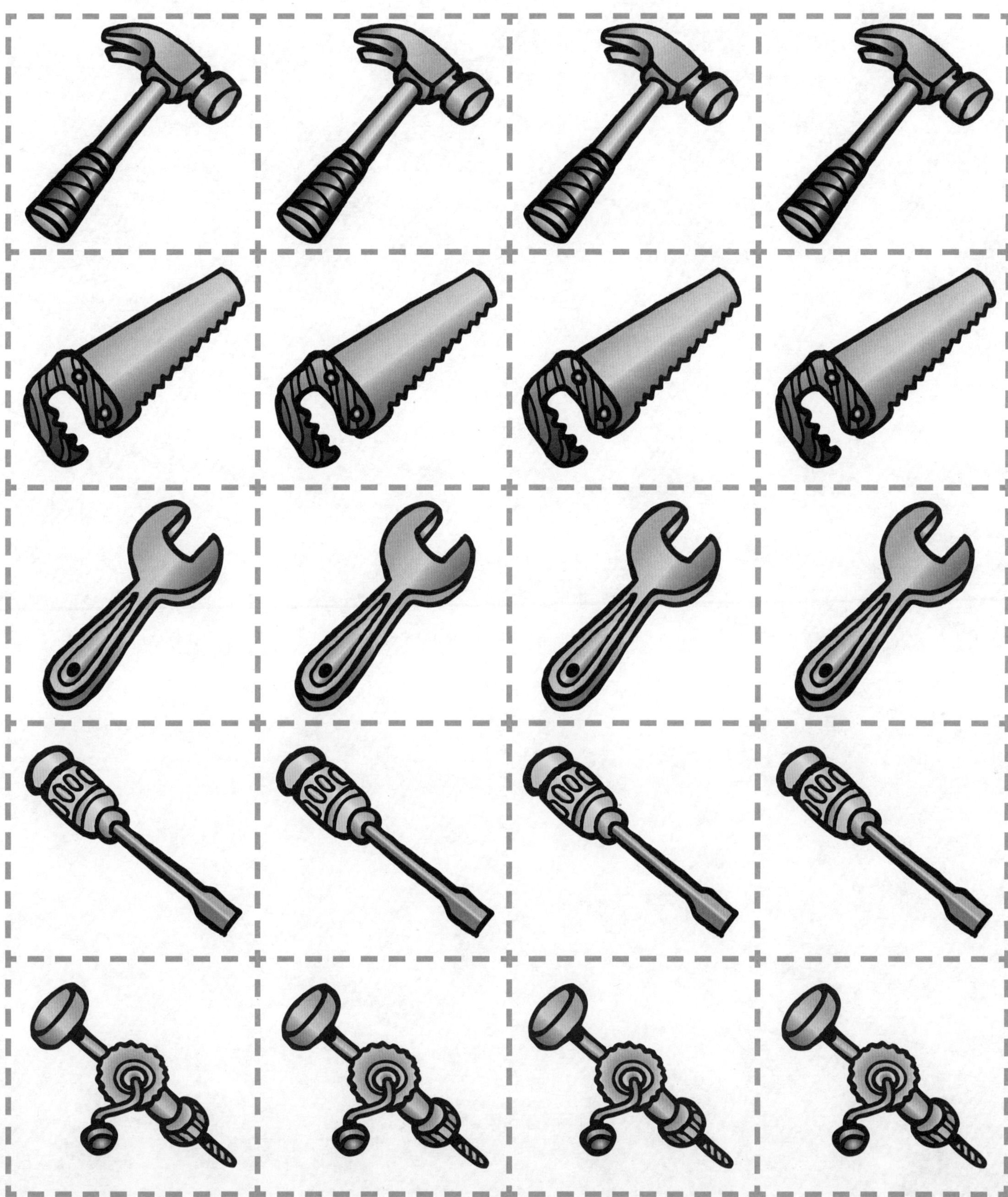

Ten Little Donuts

Standard: *Knows that the quantity of objects in a group can change by taking away some objects*

Presentation Ideas

This is a pattern song that subtracts one number with each verse.

Cut out and laminate the colored donuts (pages 45 and 47) and the numeral cards (page 7). Place ten donuts in the pocket chart. Before singing, have the class count the donuts out loud. Place the numeral card for 10 next to the donuts.

Sing the song for students. When you get to "…grabbed one donut and took it away," remove one donut from the pocket chart. Ask students, "How many donuts are left in the bakery?" and lead the students in counting the remaining donuts out loud. Replace the numeral 10 with the card for 9. Sing the song again, starting with nine little donuts. Repeat this pattern until all of the donuts are gone, then sing, "No little donuts in the bakery shop—the end!"

Once students are familiar with the song, make it even more fun. When you sing, "Along came…" replace "a child" with a student's name and allow that student to come up and take a donut.

For individual hands-on practice, give each student a stick of ten stacking cubes and have them remove one for each verse as they sing along.

Once students are familiar with the pattern, start with any number, such as, "Six little donuts in the bakery shop…," and have students supply the number to start the next verse. This is a good exercise for learning how to "count back" from a given number.

Use the colored donuts to form subtraction equations. You will need the operation symbol cards (pages 9 and 11). Place four donuts in the pocket chart. Sing "Four little donuts in the bakery shop…" and place the numeral card for 4 underneath. When you get to, "Along came a child…", select a student to come up and take a donut. Underneath the remaining donuts, place the "–" symbol and the numeral card for 1, followed by the "=" symbol and the numeral card for 3. Explain to students that the "–" is a minus sign and it means "take away" and that this number sentence or equation reads, "Four minus one equals three."

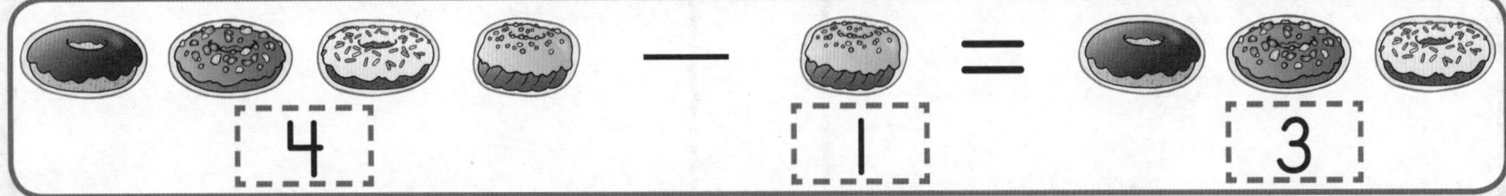

Play "What's in the Box?" to reinforce mental subtraction. Have students watch you count a few donuts and put them into a box. Then, without showing them the inside of the box, have them watch as you take one donut out of the box. Ask students, "How many donuts are in the box now?" After students answer, take the donuts out and count them to check.

The worksheet on page 42 can be used for practice or assessment. Students count the donuts in each box and write the number. Then, they draw donuts in each box at the bottom to match the numeral given. If some students are not able to draw donuts, let them make circles or dots.

Name: ______________________________

Donut Count

Directions: Count the donuts in each box and write the number in the box.

Directions: Draw the correct number of donuts in each box.

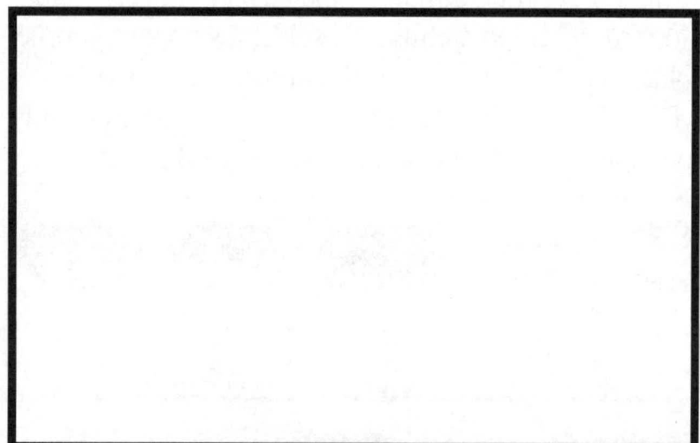

7

10

Ten Little Donuts

Ten little donuts in the bakery shop
Looking mighty yummy with the sprinkles on top.
Along came a child with a penny to pay
Grabbed that donut and took it away!

Nine little donuts in the bakery shop
Looking mighty yummy with the sprinkles on top.
Along came a child with a penny to pay
Grabbed that donut and took it away!

Eight little donuts. . .

Ten Little Donuts

Ten little donuts in the bakery shop
Looking mighty yummy with the sprinkles on top.
Along came a child with a penny to pay
Grabbed that donut and took it away!

Nine little donuts in the bakery shop
Looking mighty yummy
with the sprinkles on top.
Along came a child with a penny to pay
Grabbed that donut and took it away!

Eight little donuts. . .

Donuts

Donuts

Five Green Frogs

Standards: *Uses whole number models to represent problems*
Draws pictures to represent problems
Knows that the quantity of objects in a group can change by taking away some objects

Presentation Ideas

This is a pattern song that subtracts one number with each verse, but can be changed to an addition pattern as well.

Cut out and laminate the numeral cards (page 7) and the colored frogs, log, and pond (pages 55–59). Place the log in the pocket chart under the song, then slip five frogs into the pocket so they are in front of the log. It will look as if the frogs are "on" the log. Before singing, have the class count the frogs out loud to determine the starting number and place the appropriate numeral card next to the frogs.

Place the pond on another row of the pocket chart. Sing the song (page 53), and when you get to "One jumped into the pool," remove one frog from the log and place it behind the pond so it "disappears under the water." It is important to put the frog out of sight, so students will not count it. Ask students, "How many frogs are left on the log?" and lead the students in counting the remaining frogs out loud. Change the numeral card to the new number and finish singing, "Then there were…"

Sing the song again, moving another frog from the log to the pond, and repeat this pattern until all of the frogs are in the pond. Then sing, "No green and speckled frogs—the end!"

At first, use the numeral cards to show the counting number. Simply switch the numeral card each time you sing a new verse. As the children become better at recognizing each numeral, introduce the number word cards.

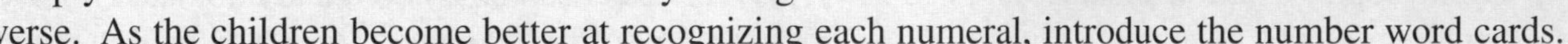

Once students are familiar with the song, extend it to addition. Change the lyrics to, "One jumped out of the pool," then take a frog out from behind the pond and place it back on the log. Recount the frogs on the log before starting the next verse.

Students can act out the song as well. Designate an area as the "pond" and line up some chairs to be the log. Ask some "frogs" (students) to sit on the "log" (chairs) as the class sings. The frogs should act out the song by jumping into or out of the pool. Remind the students that they are only to count the frogs on the log, not the frogs in the pond.

For individual hands-on practice, give each student some stacking cubes and have them remove or add one cube for each verse as they sing along.

Once students are familiar with the pattern, ask them to decide ahead of time the starting number of frogs on the log and whether a frog will jump in or out of the pool.

Five Green Frogs *(cont.)*

Presentation Ideas *(cont.)*

 Use the numeral and operation symbol cards to form equations as in the previous units (see pages 33 and 41). Place five frogs on the log in the pocket chart and place the 5 numeral card underneath. Sing the song and when you get to, "One jumped into the pool…" select a student to come up and move a frog. Underneath the remaining frogs, place the "-" symbol and the numeral card for 1, followed by the "=" symbol and the 4 numeral card. Explain to students that the "-" is a minus sign and it means "take away" and that this number sentence or equation reads, "Five minus one equals four," or "Five take away one equals four." You can do the same for addition by having frogs jump out of the pool and back onto the log, using the "+" symbol to create an equation. Help students determine if addition or subtraction is required.

 Play "What's in the Box?" as before (see pages 33 and 41) by adding or taking away frogs from the box and asking students to mentally figure how many frogs are left.

 Cut out and laminate the frog counters (pages 61 and 63). You can make extra "frog" counters by painting dried beans or small rocks green (glue on googly eyes or draw eyes with markers if you wish).

 Make copies of the worksheet on page 51. This worksheet can be colored and laminated for use with small groups or in centers. Give each student a handful of frog counters (or other small manipulatives) and ask them to place some frogs on the log. As students sing the song, have them make one of their frogs jump into the pond, and then count the frogs remaining on the log. Let students make up their own number stories about frogs and act them out on their mats.

 Once students are comfortable acting out frog stories with counters, give them their own copies of page 51. They can color their pages if they wish. Have them draw some frogs on the log, then show one jumping into or out of the pool with an arrow. At the bottom of the page, help them write the equation that goes with their story. If some students have trouble drawing frogs, give them small stickers or let them make green dots.

 Students can make mini books of the song to read and to take home. Copy pages 65–66 for each student. Students can choose the number of frogs, fill in the blanks, and draw the correct number of frogs at the end.

 The worksheet on page 52 can be used for practice or assessment.

Name ____

Jumping Frogs

Directions: Draw some frogs on the log. Draw some frogs jumping off into the water.

Directions: Write an equation to go with your drawing.

 —  = 

Name ____________________

How Many Frogs

Directions: Look at the frogs. Use the arrows to help you write equations in the boxes.

Five Green Frogs

Five green and speckled frogs
Sat on a speckled log
Eating the most delicious bugs
Yum, yum!
One jumped into the pool
Where it was nice and cool
Then there were *four* green speckled frogs
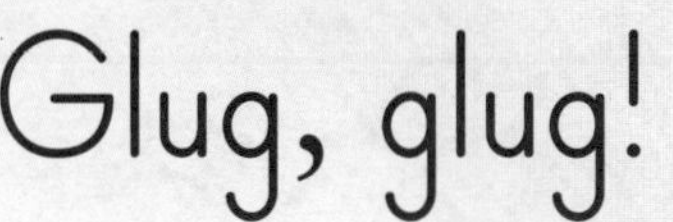
Glug, glug!

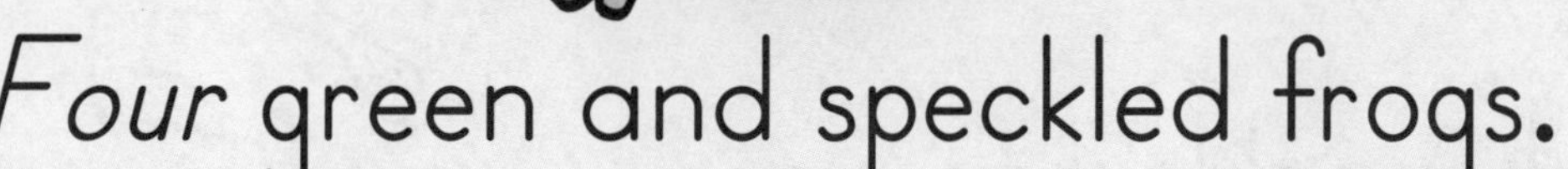
Four green and speckled frogs. . .

Five Green Frogs

Five green and speckled frogs
Sat on a speckled log
Eating the most delicious bugs
Yum, yum!
One jumped into the pool
Where it was nice and cool
Then there were *four* green speckled frogs
Glug, glug!

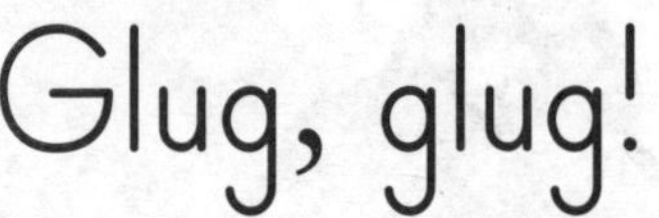

Four green and speckled frogs. . .

5 Frogs

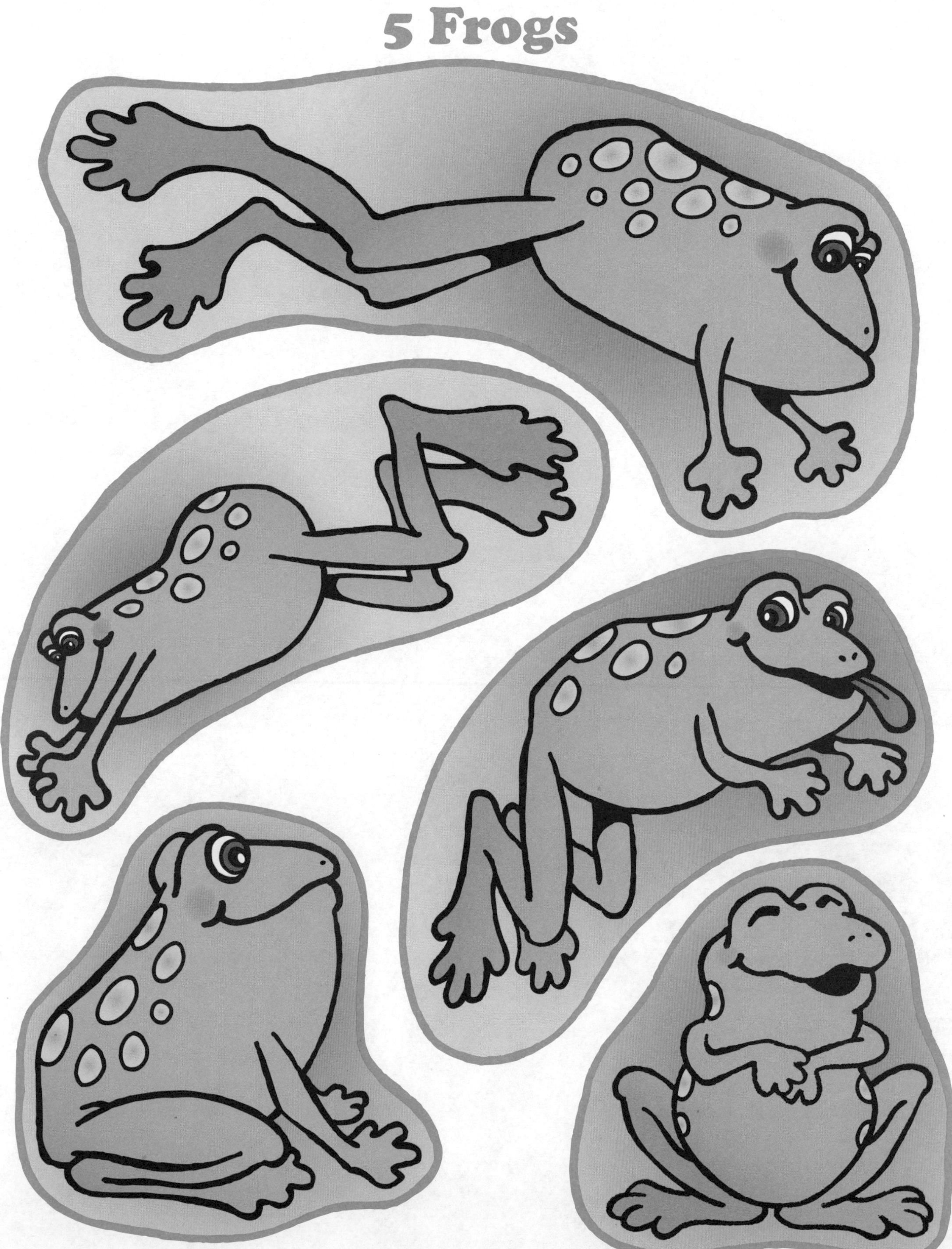

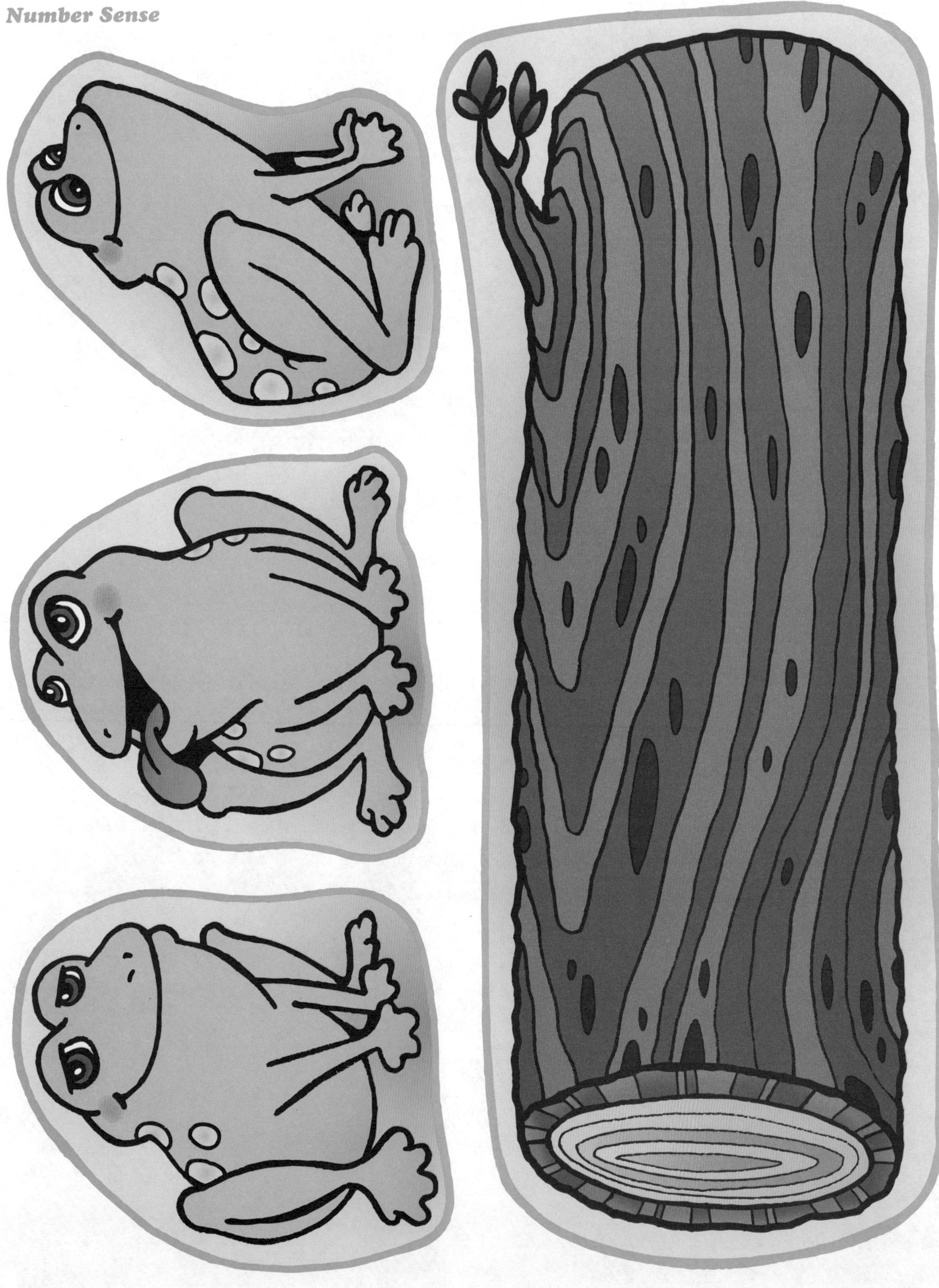

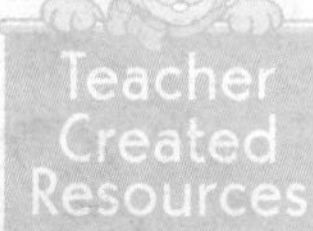

Frogs and Pond

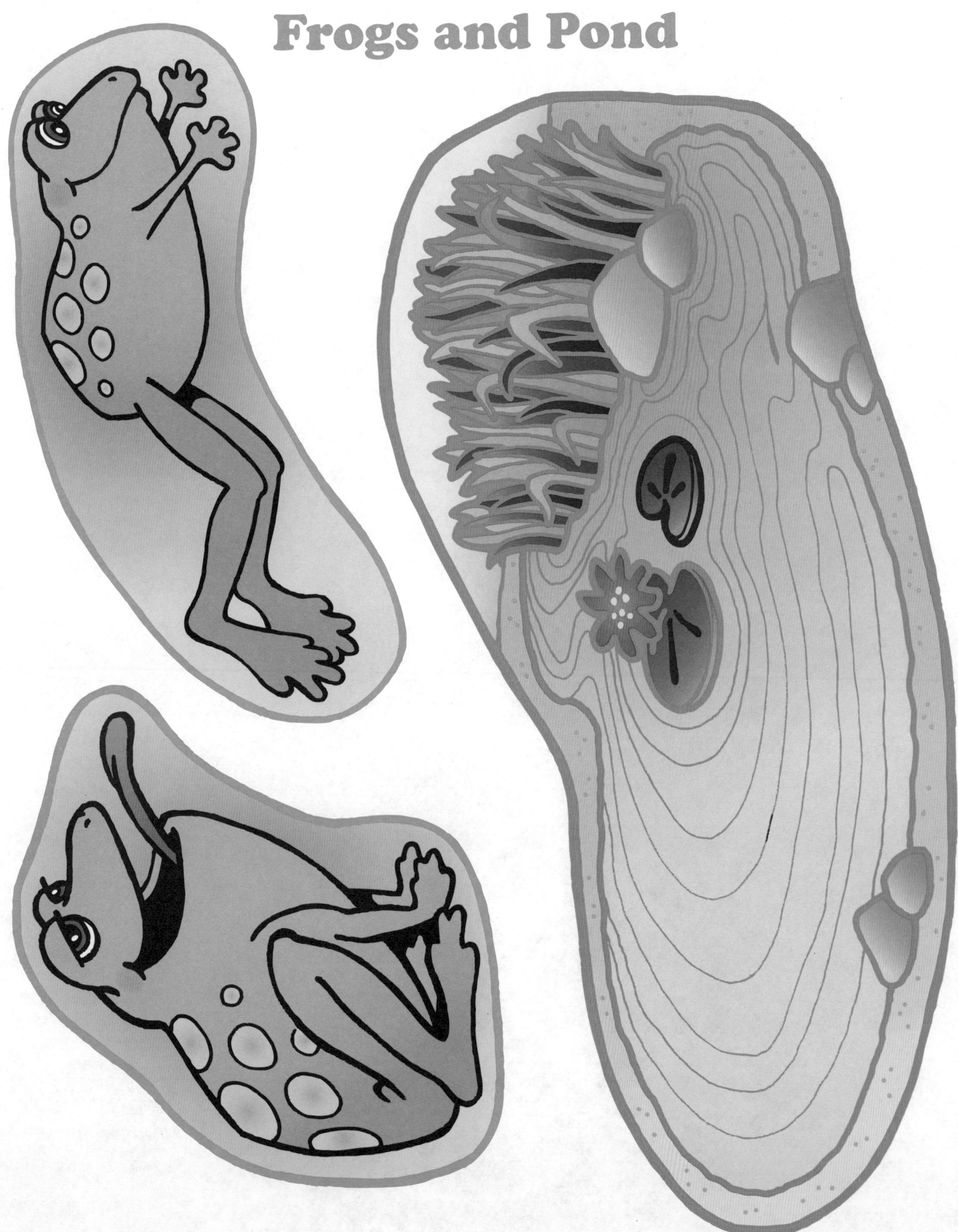

Frog Counters

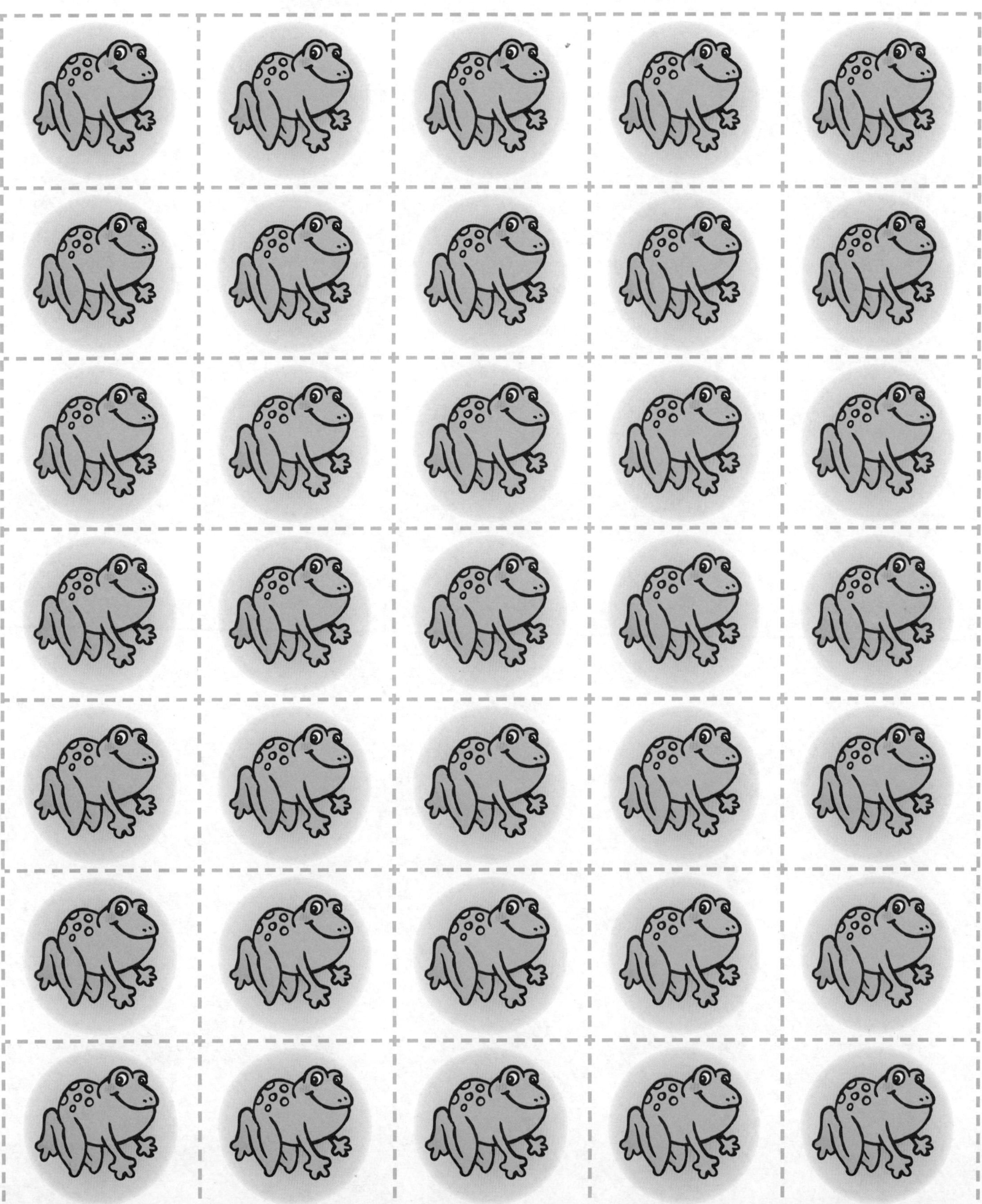

More Frog Counters

☐ Green Frogs

By ______________________________

______ green and speckled frogs sat on a speckled log eating the most delicious bugs. Yum, yum!

1

__________ jumped into the pool where it was nice and cool. 2

Then there were __________ green speckled frogs. Glug glug! 3

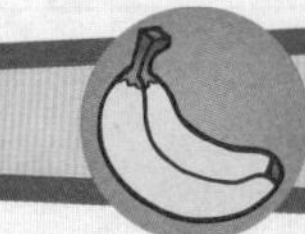

Five Little Monkeys

Standards: *Knows the common language for comparing quantity of objects (e.g., "more than," "less than," "same as")*

Understands basic whole number relationships (e.g., 4 is less than 10)

Knows that the quantity of objects in a group can change by taking away some objects

Presentation Ideas

- Cut out and laminate the monkey and crocodile puppets (pages 71 and 73) and tape craft sticks or straws onto the backs for handles.

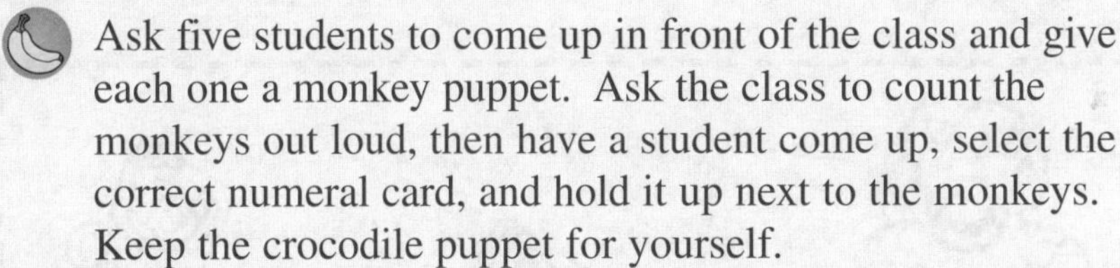

- Ask five students to come up in front of the class and give each one a monkey puppet. Ask the class to count the monkeys out loud, then have a student come up, select the correct numeral card, and hold it up next to the monkeys. Keep the crocodile puppet for yourself.

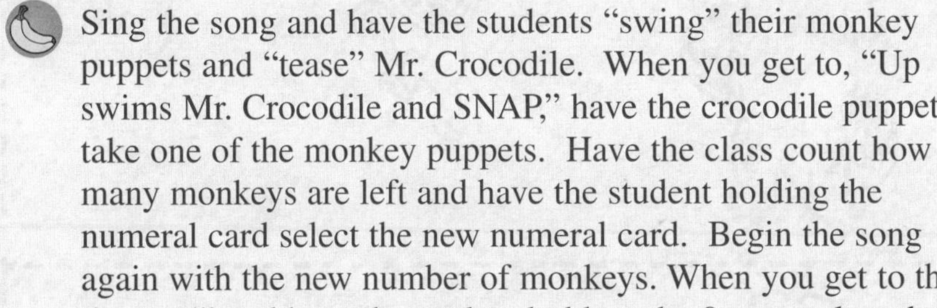

- Sing the song and have the students "swing" their monkey puppets and "tease" Mr. Crocodile. When you get to, "Up swims Mr. Crocodile and SNAP," have the crocodile puppet take one of the monkey puppets. Have the class count how many monkeys are left and have the student holding the numeral card select the new numeral card. Begin the song again with the new number of monkeys. When you get to the end, sing, "No little monkeys swinging in the tree!" and have the student hold up the 0 numeral card.

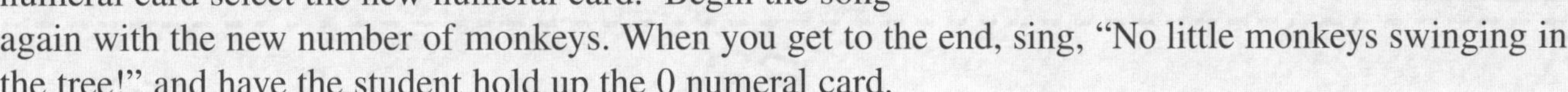

- Students can also act out the song using the monkey and crocodile masks on page 75 and 76. Let students color and cut out their masks, then attach string or ribbon to tie them on. Don't forget to make eyeholes!

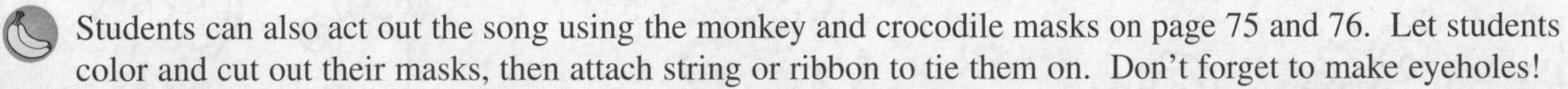

- Once students are familiar with the song, let them choose how many monkeys will get snapped up, then figure how many are left. Or, draw a number card or roll a die to see how many get snapped up. Use the numeral and operations symbol cards to show the proper equations (see pages 33, 41, or 50 for directions).

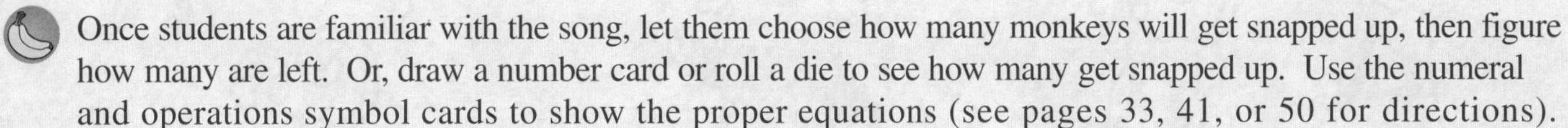

- To work on comparing quantities, play the Greedy Alligator game. Give monkey puppets to students and have some stand on each side of you. Tell students that Mr. Crocodile is very greedy and wants to eat the bigger group of monkeys. Have students count the monkeys on your left and then the monkeys on your right and make a verbal comparison, "Three is less than five. Five is more than three." Emphasize the terms more than, less than, and equal. The students can tell Mr. Crocodile which group he should eat. Then, of course, Mr. Crocodile can "eat" the bigger group. If the groups are equal, he can eat both! Make extra copies of the monkey puppets and try the activity with larger groups.

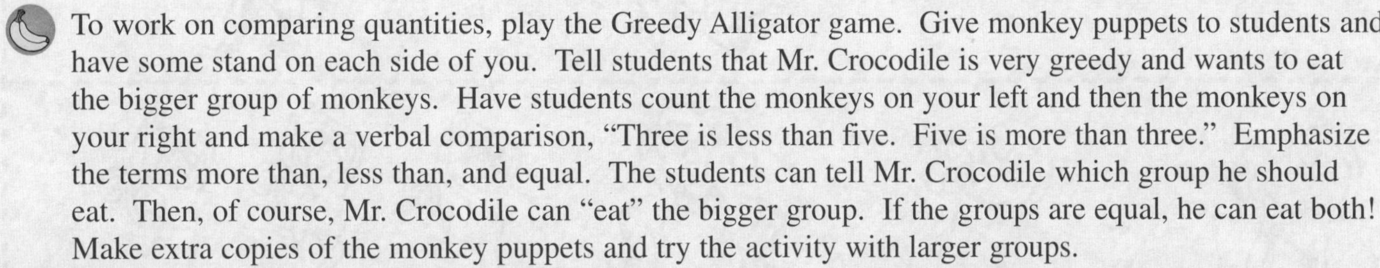

- Students can make mini books of the song to read and to take home. Copy pages 77 and 78 for each student. Students can choose the number of monkeys, fill in the blanks, and draw the correct number of monkeys.

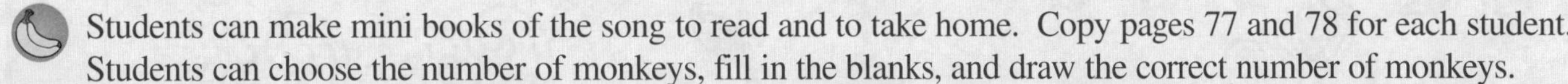

- The worksheet on page 68 can be used for practice or assessment.

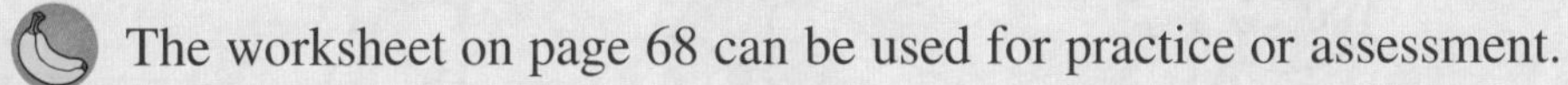

Name ______________________________

More Monkeys

Directions: Circle the larger group of monkeys in each row.

Five Little Monkeys

Five little monkeys
Swinging in a tree
Teasing Mr. Crocodile
You can't catch me
Along comes Mr. Crocodile
As quiet as can be, and SNAP

Four little monkeys...

Three little monkeys...

Two little monkeys...

One little monkey...

No little monkeys
swinging in a tree!

Five Little Monkeys

Five little monkeys
Swinging in a tree
Teasing Mr. Crocodile
You can't catch me
Along comes Mr. Crocodile
As quiet as can be, and SNAP

Four little monkeys...

Three little monkeys...

Two little monkeys...

One little monkey...

No little monkeys
swinging in a tree!

Monkeys

Monkey and Crocodile

Monkey Mask

Crocodile Mask

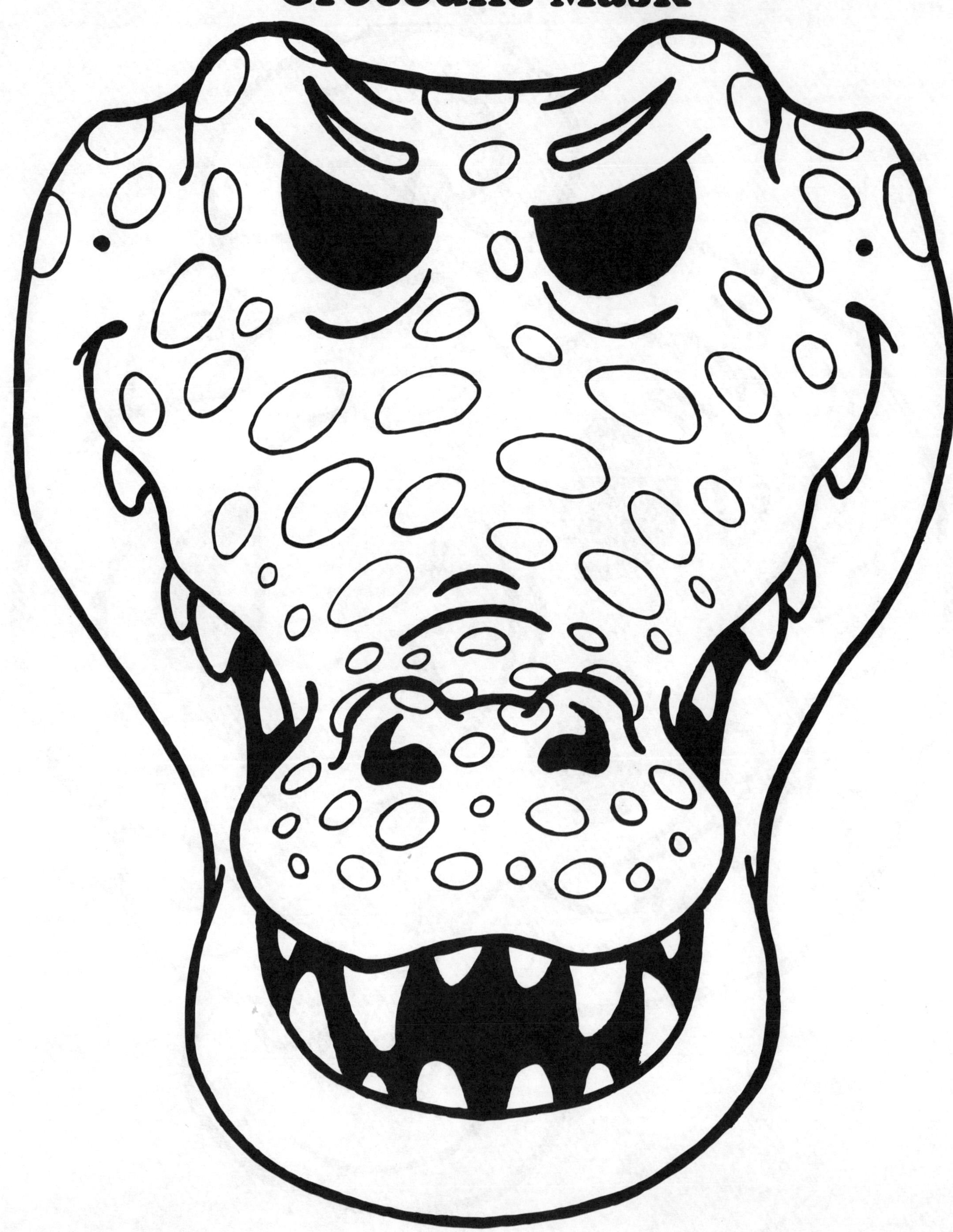

Little Monkeys
by
little monkeys swinging in a tree.
Teasing Mr. Crocodile, You can't catch me!
1

Along swims Mr. Crocodile as quiet as can be and SNAP!

__________ little monkeys swinging in a tree! 3

Algebra—Patterning

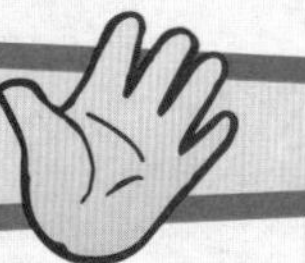

Standards: Understands simple patterns; Repeats simple patterns; Extends simple patterns

Presentation Ideas

Young students need a great deal of practice recognizing, repeating, and extending patterns. Because young children learn effectively through physical activity, the song "Head, Shoulders, Knees, and Toes" makes a perfect springboard for patterning activities.

Cut out and laminate the movement picture cards (pages 83–91). Use these movements to practice patterning with your students before introducing the song. Begin with the simplest pattern (ABABAB) by choosing only two movement cards and alternating them (head, shoulders, head, shoulders…) in a pocket chart. Lead students in repeating the pattern while doing the movements. Ask students to predict what movement comes next and add more cards to extend the pattern.

Choose (or let students choose) two more movement cards to create another pattern (jump, clap, jump, clap…) having students chant the pattern while doing the movements, then predict what comes next and extend the pattern. Use the movement cards to create and extend many different ABAB patterns over several days until students are comfortable with the process.

Once students are accomplished at creating and extending ABAB patterns, add a third movement card to make the pattern more complicated (head, shoulders, knees, head shoulders, knees…). Have students chant the pattern while doing the movements, then predict and extend the pattern. As students get more skilled at patterning, you can create more complicated patterns (ABCDABCD, ABBABB, AABAAB, etc.) for them to predict and extend. Let students create their own patterns for the class to chant and perform.

The song "Head, Shoulders, Knees, and Toes" contains an ABCDCD ABCDCD pattern. When students are comfortable with patterns containing four elements, introduce the song by placing the movement cards for the first two lines ("Head, shoulders, knees and toes, knees and toes") in a pocket chart. Examine the pattern with students and ask them to predict the next line. Practice the pattern by chanting the words and doing the movements.

Explain to students that part of the song uses the pattern, but not the entire song. Put the movement cards for the entire song in the pocket chart and sing it for students, then have the class sing the song and do the movements with you, one verse at a time.

Once students are comfortable with the first three verses, you can extend the song by choosing other movements and creating your own verses. Don't worry if it doesn't rhyme—the idea is to practice patterning.

The cut-and-paste worksheet on page 80 can be used for practice or assessment.

Name ____________________

What's Next?

Directions: Cut out the children on the right side of the page and glue them into the correct pattern.

Head, Shoulders, Knees, and Toes

Head, shoulders, knees, and toes
Knees and toes
Head, shoulders, knees, and toes
Knees and toes
And eyes and ears and mouth and nose
Head, shoulders, knees and toes
Knees and toes

Wrists, elbows, chest and hips
Chest and hips
Wrists, elbows, chest and hips
Chest and hips
Eyebrows, cheeks, and teeth and lips
Wrists, elbows, chest and hips
Chest and hips

Jump, wave, stomp, and clap
Stomp and clap
Jump, wave, stomp, and clap
Stomp and clap
Spin and bow and snap, snap, snap
Jump, wave, stomp and clap
Stomp and clap

Head, Shoulders, Knees, and Toes

Head, shoulders, knees, and toes
Knees and toes
Head, shoulders, knees, and toes
Knees and toes
And eyes and ears and mouth and nose
Head, shoulders, knees and toes
Knees and toes

Wrists, elbows, chest and hips
Chest and hips
Wrists, elbows, chest and hips
Chest and hips
Eyebrows, cheeks, and teeth and lips
Wrists, elbows, chest and hips
Chest and hips

Jump, wave, stomp, and clap
Stomp and clap
Jump, wave, stomp, and clap
Stomp and clap
Spin and bow and snap, snap, snap
Jump, wave, stomp and clap
Stomp and clap

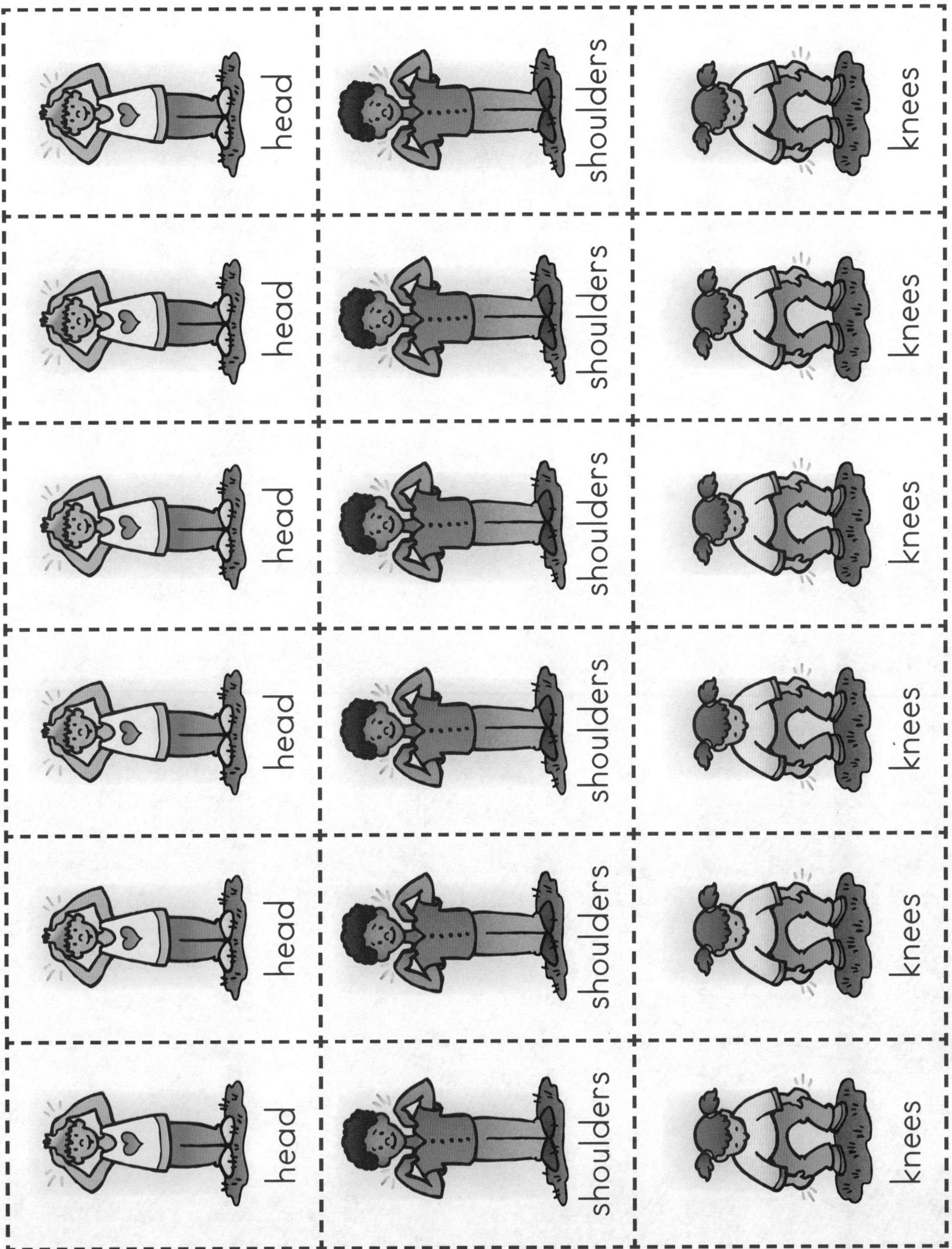
head
shoulders
knees
head
shoulders
knees
head
shoulders
knees
head
shoulders
knees
head
shoulders
knees
head
shoulders
knees

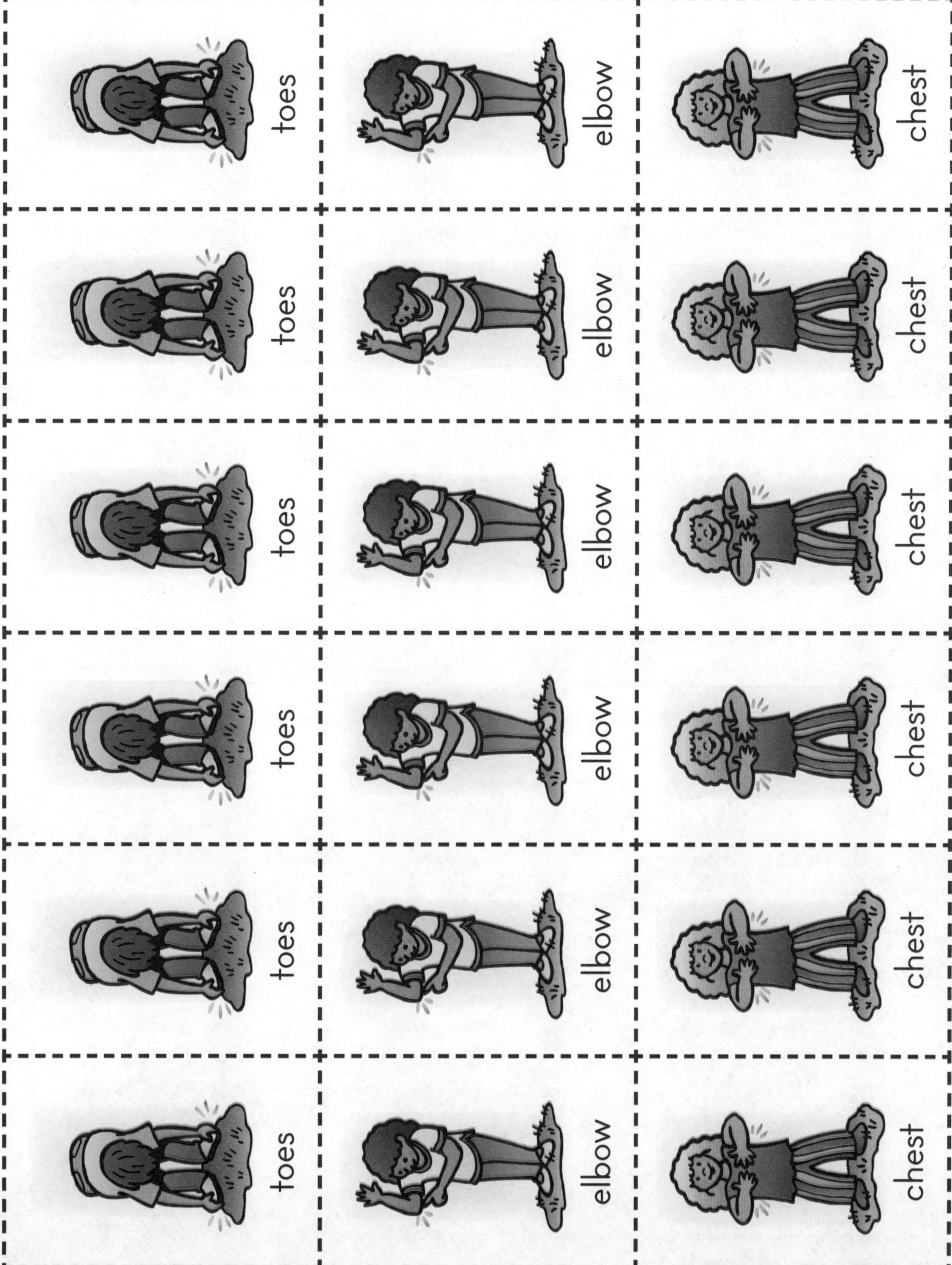
toes
elbow
chest
toes
elbow
chest
toes
elbow
chest
toes
elbow
chest
toes
elbow
chest
toes
elbow
chest

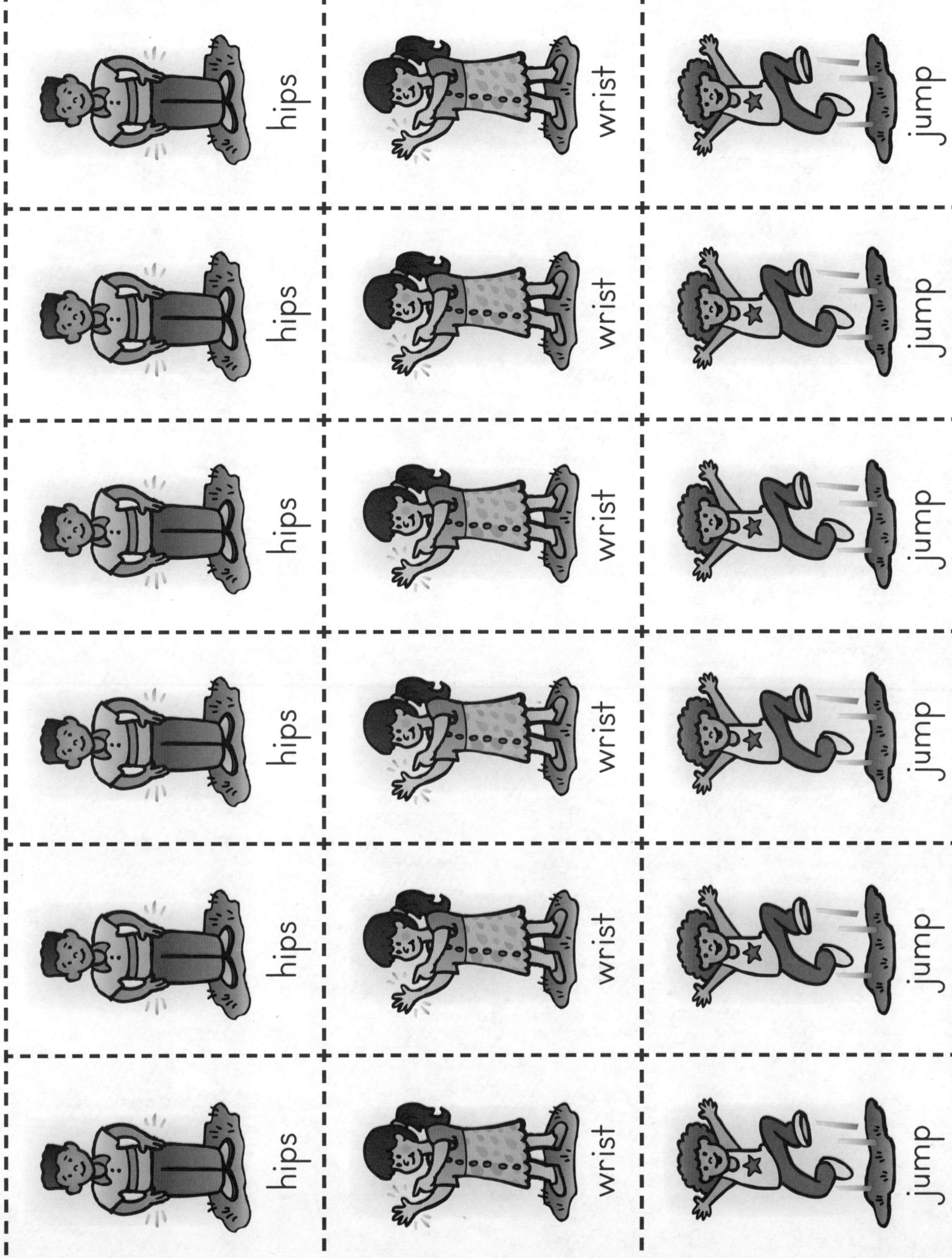
hips
wrist
jump
hips
wrist
jump
hips
wrist
jump
hips
wrist
jump
hips
wrist
jump
hips
wrist
jump

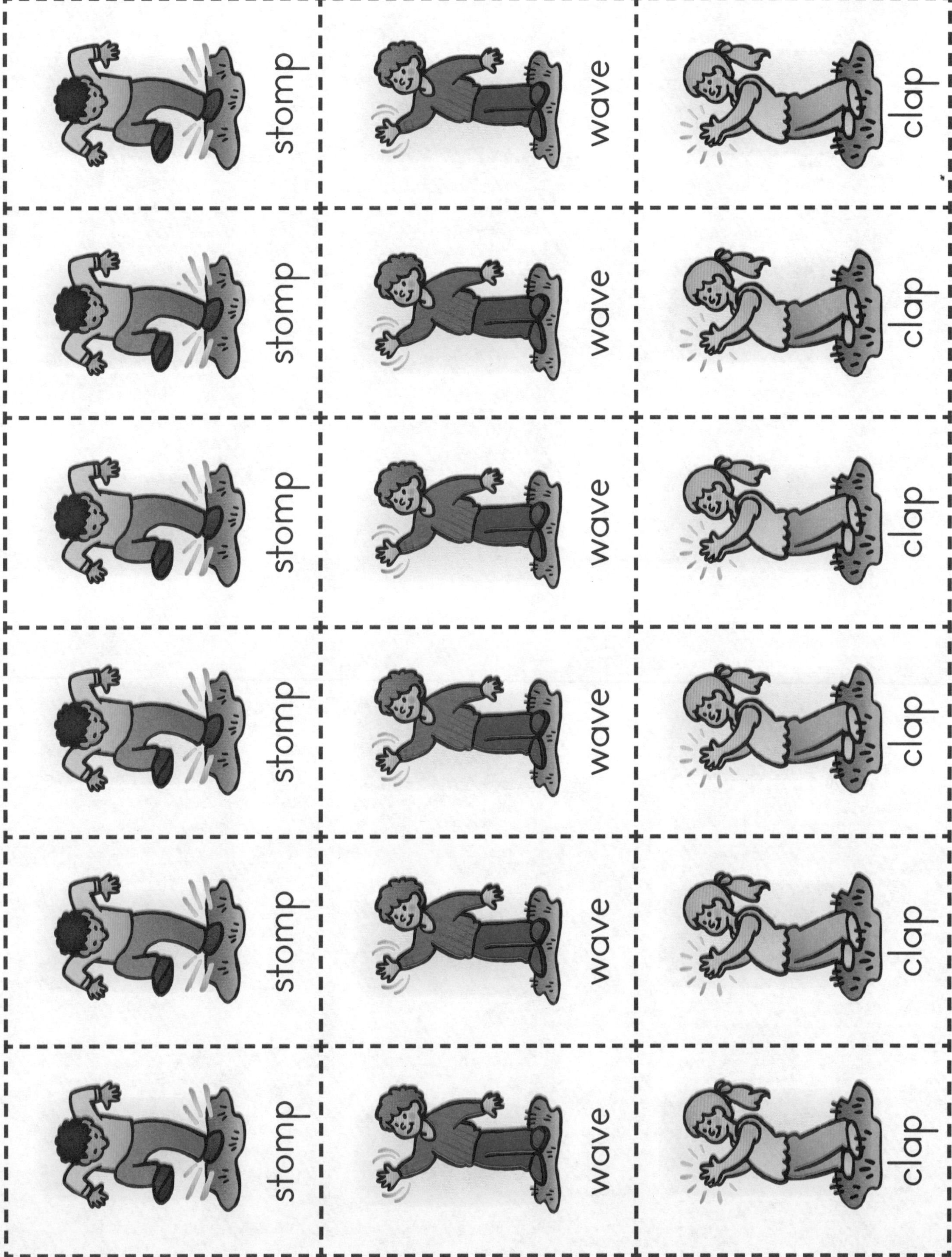
stomp
wave
clap
stomp
wave
clap
stomp
wave
clap
stomp
wave
clap
stomp
wave
clap
stomp
wave
clap

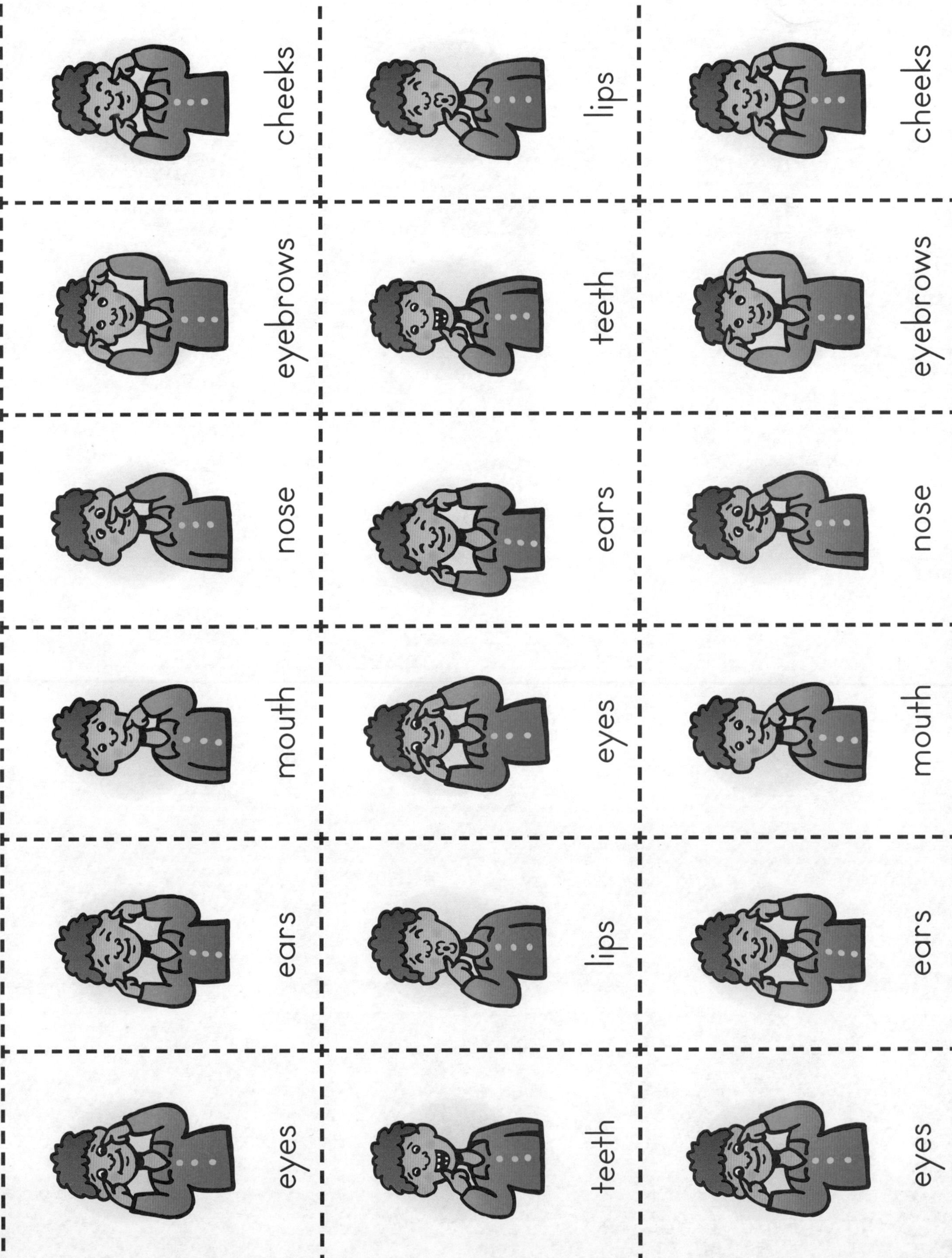
cheeks
lips
cheeks
eyebrows
teeth
eyebrows
nose
ears
nose
mouth
eyes
mouth
ears
lips
ears
eyes
teeth
eyes

Days of the Week

Standard: Understands the concept of a calendar, a day, a week, a month, a year

Presentation Ideas

Tell students that they will be learning about the days of the week. Ask if anyone knows what a *day* is. Guide students to understand that for them a day begins when they get up in the morning and ends while they are sleeping. (When they wake up the next morning, a *new* day has started.)

Copy, cut out, and laminate the *Days of the Week Cards* (pages 94–96).

Explain that to keep track of time people put days into groups called weeks. Each week has seven days, and each one has a name. Beginning with Sunday, show students each Day-of-the-Week card, read it aloud, and have students repeat it. Place each card in the pocket chart below the one before, forming a column. Read and have students repeat each day (in order) several times. Point out that when Saturday ends, the next day is Sunday and the cycle starts over again.

Once students have become familiar with the days of the week, sing the Days of the Week Song, pointing to each day of the week as you sing it. Sing the song again and have students sing and clap along with you. Continue to sing the song throughout the year to reinforce the order of the days of the week.

	Sunday
	Monday
Yesterday was	Tuesday
Today is	Wednesday
Tomorrow will be	Thursday
	Friday
	Saturday

Introduce the concepts of *today, yesterday,* and *tomorrow*. Place the days of the week cards in a vertical column in a pocket chart, leaving room on the left for more cards. Ask if anyone knows what day of the week it is today. Place the *Today is* card to the left of the current day of the week. Place the *Yesterday was* and *Tomorrow will be* cards next to the appropriate days. Have students repeat after you, "Yesterday was (fill in), today is (fill in), and tomorrow will be (fill in)." Repeat this exercise over several days until students are familiar with the process.

Once students are familiar with *today, yesterday,* and *tomorrow,* introduce the song *Today Is*. Sing this song daily to reinforce students' understanding of the days of the week.

Cut out and laminate the one-month color calendar (page 101) and color-coded day of the week squares (page 103). Hang the calendar where students can see it and write in the numbers for the current month. Each day, have a student select a color-coded square and place it on the calendar for the current day. This exercise will give students a visual representation of the repetition of the days of the week over a whole month.

Sunday	Monday	Tuesday	Wednesday	Thursday	Friday	Saturday
Sunday	Monday	Tuesday	Wednesday	Thursday	Friday	Saturday
Sunday	Monday	Tuesday	Wednesday	Thursday	Friday	Saturday
Sunday	Monday	Tuesday	Wednesday	Thursday	Friday	Saturday
Sunday	Monday	Tuesday	Wednesday	Thursday	Friday	Saturday
Sunday	Monday	Tuesday	Wednesday	Thursday	Friday	Saturday

Monday

Tuesday

Saturday

Friday

Sunday

Thursday

Wednesday

Yesterday was

Today is

Tomorrow will be

Days of the Week Song

(Try singing to the tune of "The Addams Family" theme song.)

Days of the week
clap, clap
Days of the week
clap, clap
Days of the week
Days of the week
Days of the week
clap, clap

There's Sunday and there's Monday
There's Tuesday and there's Wednesday
There's Thursday and there's Friday
And then there's Saturday

Days of the Week Song

(Try singing to the tune of "The Addams Family" theme song.)

Days of the week
clap, clap
Days of the week
clap, clap
Days of the week
Days of the week
Days of the week
clap, clap

There's Sunday and there's Monday
There's Tuesday and there's Wednesday
There's Thursday and there's Friday
And then there's Saturday

Today Is

(Try singing to the tune of "Frere Jácques.")

Today is *Tuesday*
Today is *Tuesday*
All day long, all day long
Yesterday was *Monday*
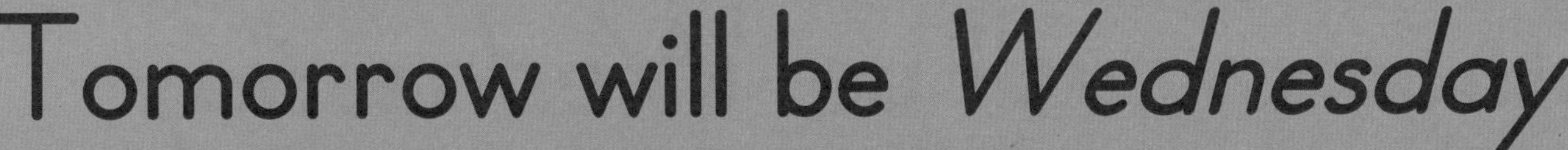
Tomorrow will be *Wednesday*
Oh, what fun! Sing along!

Today Is

(Try singing to the tune of "Frere Jácques.")

Today is *Tuesday*
Today is *Tuesday*
All day long, all day long
Yesterday was *Monday*

Tomorrow will be *Wednesday*
Oh, what fun! Sing along!

Sunday	Monday	Tuesday	Wednesday	Thursday	Friday	Saturday

Directions: Laminate and cut out these cards for use with the calendar on page 101.

Sunday	Monday	Tuesday	Wednesday	Thursday	Friday	Saturday
Sunday	Monday	Tuesday	Wednesday	Thursday	Friday	Saturday
Sunday	Monday	Tuesday	Wednesday	Thursday	Friday	Saturday
Sunday	Monday	Tuesday	Wednesday	Thursday	Friday	Saturday
Sunday	Monday	Tuesday	Wednesday	Thursday	Friday	Saturday

Months of the Year

Standard: Understands the concept of a calendar, a day, a week, a month, a year

Presentation Ideas

Show students a commercially-produced monthly calendar. As you flip through the pages, explain that this type of calendar shows every day for a whole year—365 days in all. Because that's a lot of days to keep straight, we divide the year into twelve months.

Tell students that to learn the names of the months of the year, they will chant a rhyme about birthdays. They will need to know what month their birthday falls in. Be prepared to tell some students what their birth month is if they do not know.

- Copy, cut out, and laminate the Months of the Year Cards (pages 106–108) and place them in a pocket chart in order.
- Tell students that you will say a rhyme and then call out the name of each month. When they hear the month that their birthday is in, they should stand up. When you call out the following month, they should sit down.
- Read the *Apples, Peaches, Pears, Plums* chant (page 109) and then slowly call out each month in order. You may need to prompt students at first; "Okay, everyone whose birthday is in January should stand up now." As students become familiar with the chant, have them chant along with you and call out the months.
- Teach students the song "These Are the Months of the Year" (page 111). Sing the song often to practice and reinforce the order of the months.
- Create a birthday graph for your class. Cut out and laminate the colored *Birthday Graph* (pages 114–115). Have each student write his or her name in a space above their birthday month. You could also make small copies of students' photos and have them stick the photos on the graph. When the graph is complete, discuss it with students.

Sample questions: Which month has the most birthdays? Which month has the lowest number of birthdays? Are there more birthdays in June or October?

Happy Birthday

	January	February	March	April	May	June	July	August	September	October	November	December
7												
6												
5			Temo					Griff		Mo		
4	Ivar		Tal				Raphael	Javier		Drake	Anelle	
3	Albino		Maria	Eric			Grutle	Rufus		Boris	Siran	
2	Pedro	Ralph	Drew	Marco		Rune	Yao	Rollo		Ramses	Benicio	Hollis
1	Hajir	Tony	Carey	Ferny	Klaus	Bjorn	Lemmy	Angel	Nev	Shiva	Loki	Kitty

- Give each student a sheet of paper. Ask students to write or dictate their birth date and create an illustration showing what they would like to do or have done in the past on their birthdays. Collect the pages into a class book—arrange the pages in order by month.

January

February

April

March

June

May

August

July

September

October

November

December

Apples, Peaches, Pears, Plums

Apples, peaches,
Pears, plums
Tell me when
Your birthday comes.

January
February
March
April
May
June
July
August
September
October
November
December

Apples, Peaches, Pears, Plums

Apples, peaches,
Pears, plums
Tell me when
Your birthday comes.

January
February
March
April
May
June
July
August
September
October
November
December

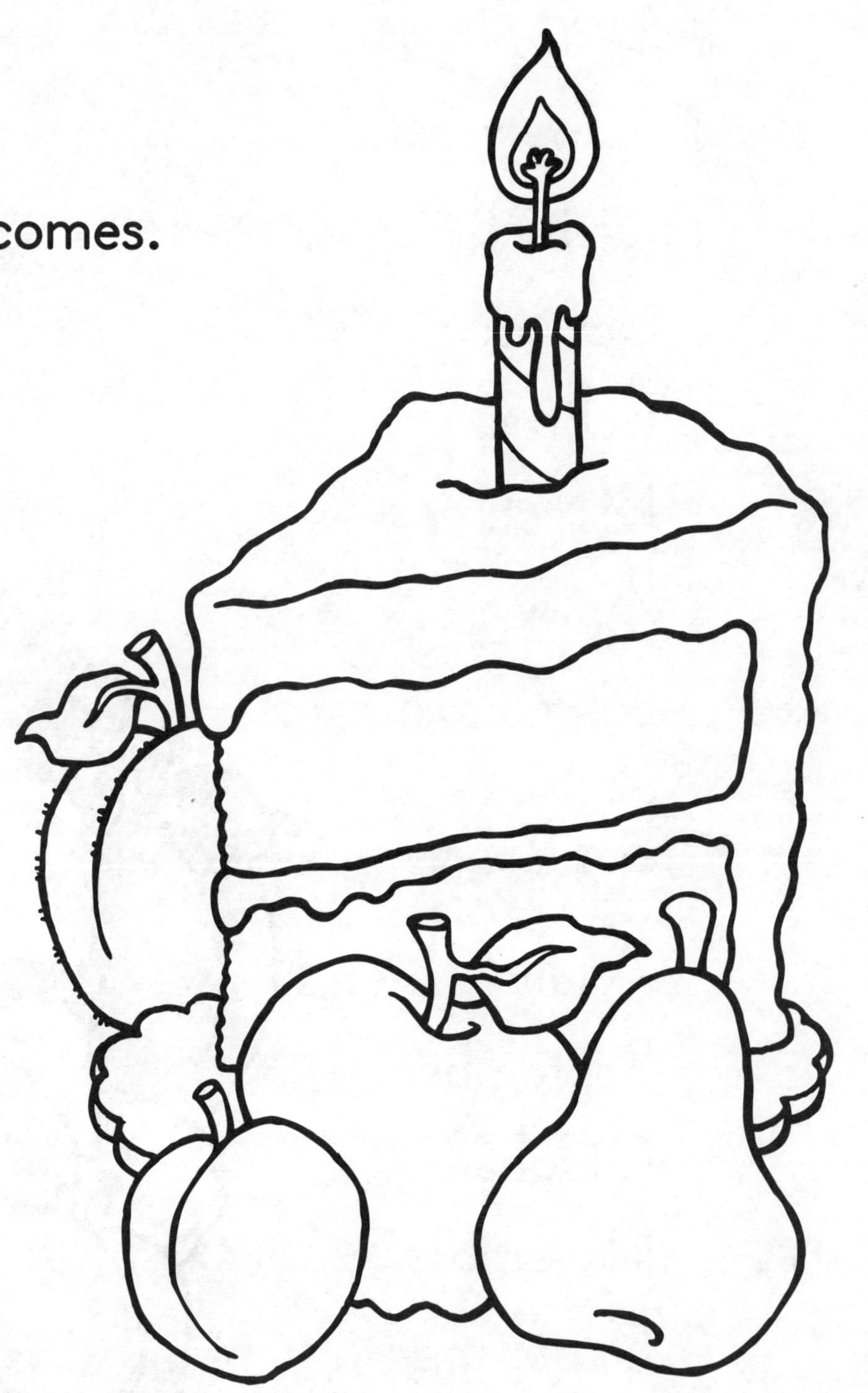

These Are the Months of the Year

(Try singing to the tune of "Ten Little Indians.")

January, February, March, and April
May and June and July and August
September, October, November, December
These are the months of the year.

These Are the Months of the Year

(Try singing to the tune of "Ten Little Indians.")

January, February, March, and April
May and June and July and August
September, October, November, December
These are the months of the year.

Happy
7
6
5
4
3
2
1
January
February
March
April
May
June

Birthday
July
August
September
October
November
December

Ordering

Standards: *Knows the common language of measurement (e.g., big, little, long, short, light, heavy)*
Orders objects qualitatively by measurable attribute
(e.g., smallest to largest, lightest to heaviest, shortest to longest)

Presentation Ideas

Cut out and laminate the puppets for "Goldilocks and the Three Bears" and "The Three Billy Goats Gruff" (pages 131–137, 151–153). Tape craft sticks or straws to the back to create handles. Use the puppets to tell each story (page 118 and page 139) to students. Emphasize the measurement concepts, which are printed in blue text, as you read each story. Use appropriate voices for each character to reinforce their size—have fun!

On subsequent readings, let students hold the puppets and act out the story as you read. As they become more familiar with the stories students can say the characters' lines along with you.

To practice the language of measurement, have students line up the bear or goat puppets by size. Talk about comparative language; What are some other words for "big"? (large, huge) What are some other ways to say "little"? (small, wee, tiny) What are some other ways we could put the bears/goats in order? (by weight, by length or height, by age)

For "Goldilocks and the Three Bears," cut out and laminate the bears, bowls, chairs, and beds (pages 131–137). Students can use these manipulatives to practice putting items in size order. Have students use standard (rulers) and non-standard (blocks or paper clips) measures to measure each item and put them in length order.

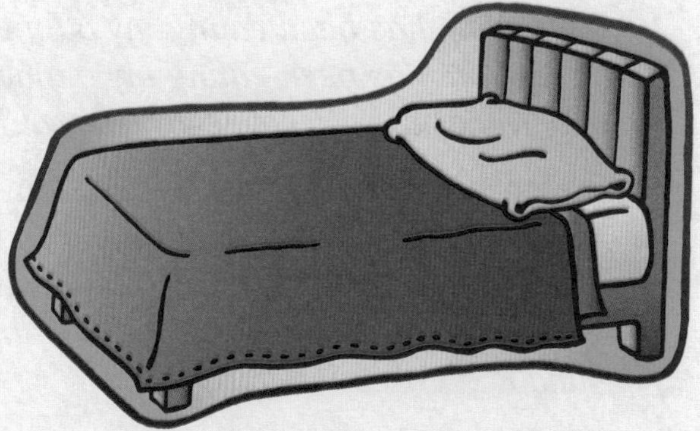

Copy the mini book pages for each student (pages 120–130 and 140–149). Cut the pages on the dotted lines and assemble them into mini books for each student. Read the stories aloud to the class as they read along in their own mini books. Students can color the illustrations and take the mini books home to share with their families.

The worksheets on pages 119 and 150 can be used for practice or assessment.

Goldilocks and the Three Bears

Once upon a time there were three bears who lived in a small house in the woods: a great, big poppa bear, a middle-sized momma bear, and a wee, little baby bear.

One morning Mama made some oatmeal for breakfast, but it was too hot to eat. The three bears went for a walk in the woods while they waited for the oatmeal to cool. Along came a little girl named Goldilocks. She saw the Bear family's cute little house and let herself inside.

She found three bowls of oatmeal on the breakfast table: a great big bowl, a middle-sized bowl, and a wee, little bowl.

She tasted the oatmeal in the big bowl. *"This one is too hot."*
She tasted the oatmeal in the middle-sized bowl. *"This one is too cold."*
She tasted the oatmeal in the small bowl. *"This one is just right."*
And she ate it all up!

Goldilocks found three chairs in the living room: a great, big chair, a middle-sized chair, and a wee, little chair.

She sat on the big chair. *"This one is too hard."*
She sat on the middle-sized chair. *"This one is too soft."*
She sat on the small chair. *"This one is just right."*
And she broke the little chair all to pieces!

She went upstairs and found three beds: a great, big bed, a middle-sized bed, and a wee, little bed.

She lay on the big bed. *"This one is too hard."*
She lay on the middle-sized bed. *"This one is too soft."*
She lay on the small bed. *"This one is just right."*

And she fell fast asleep. The three bears came home to eat their oatmeal.

"Someone has been eating my oatmeal," said Poppa in a great big voice.
"Someone has been eating my oatmeal," said Momma in a middle-sized voice.
"Someone has been eating my oatmeal," said the baby bear, in a wee, little voice, *"and it's all gone!"*

The three bears went into the living room.

"Someone has been sitting in my chair," said Poppa in a great big voice.
"Someone has been sitting in my chair," said Momma in a middle-sized voice.
"Someone has been sitting in my chair," said the baby bear in a wee, little voice, *"and it's broken into pieces!"*

The three bears went upstairs.

"Someone has been sleeping in my bed," said Poppa in a great big voice.
"Someone has been sleeping in my bed," said Momma in a middle-sized voice.
"Someone has been sleeping in my bed," said the baby bear in a wee, little voice, *"and there she is!"*

Goldilocks woke up and saw the three bears.
She ran away and never went back! —**The End**

Name: ______________________________

Goldilocks and the Three Bears

Directions: Cut on the dotted lines. Glue each picture in the correct space to show three items in size order.

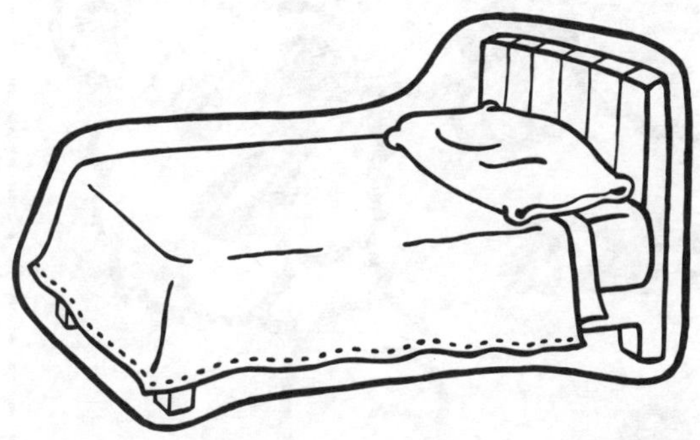

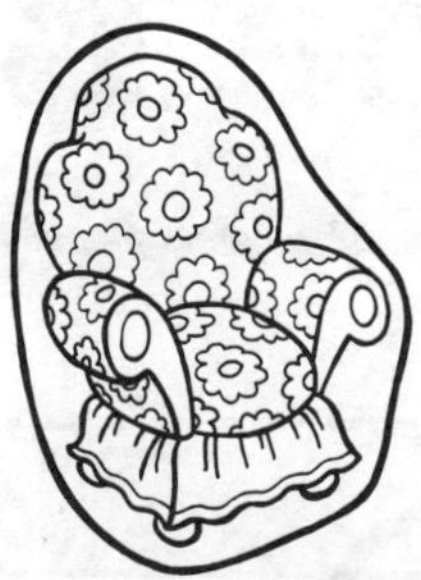

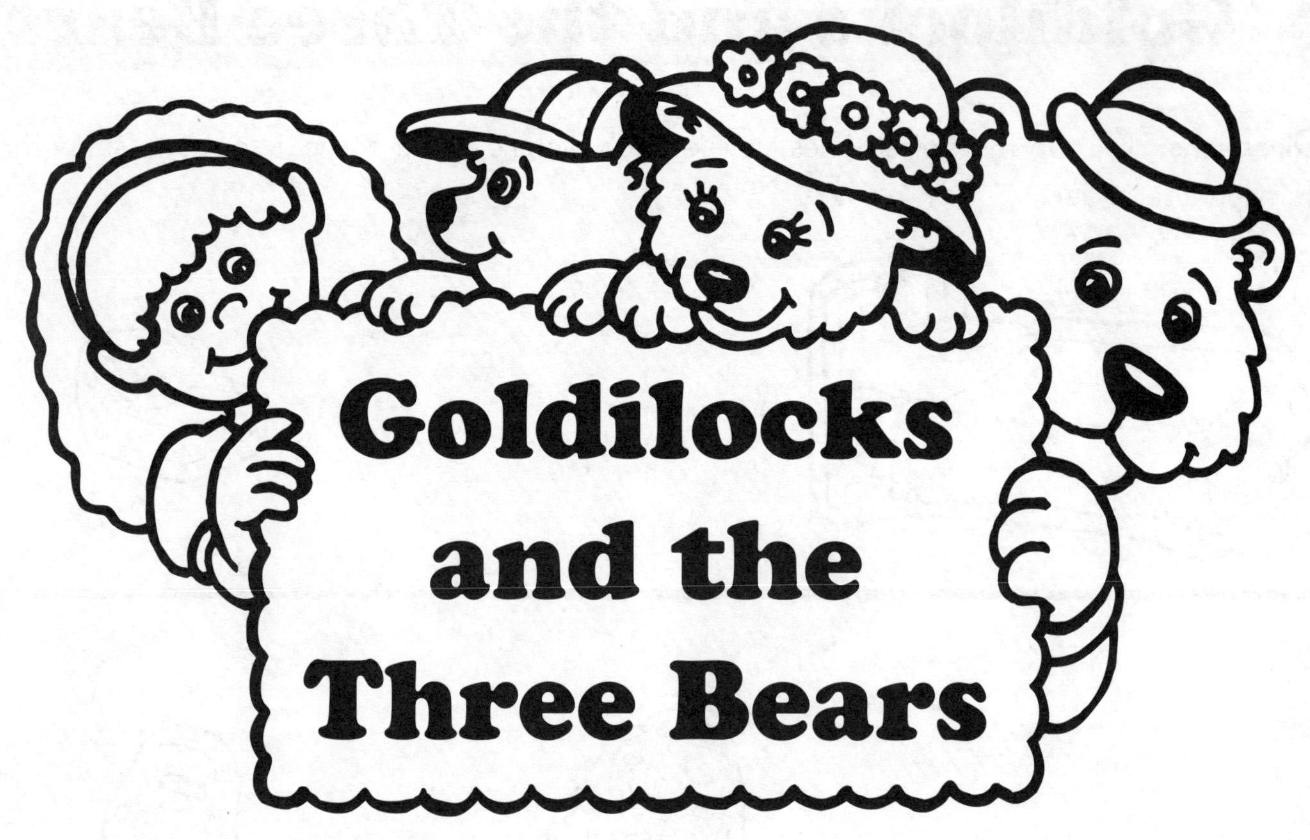

Once upon a time there were three bears who lived in a small house in the woods. 1

There was a great, big poppa bear,
a middle–sized momma bear,
and a wee, little baby bear.

2

One morning Momma made some oatmeal for breakfast, but it was too hot to eat. The three bears went for a walk in the woods while they waited for the oatmeal to cool.

3

Along came a little girl named Goldilocks. She saw the Bear family's cute little house and let herself inside.

4

She found three bowls of oatmeal on the breakfast table. There was a great big bowl, a middle-sized bowl, and a wee, little bowl.

5

She tasted the oatmeal in the big bowl.
"This one is too hot."
She tasted the oatmeal in the middle-sized bowl.
"This one is too cold."

6

She tasted the oatmeal in the small bowl.
"This one is just right." And she ate it all up!

7

Goldilocks found three chairs in the living room. She saw a great, big chair, a middle–sized chair, and a wee, little chair.

She sat on the big chair. "This one is too hard."
She sat on the middle–sized chair.
"This one is too soft."
She sat on the small chair. "This one is just right."

And she broke the little chair all to pieces! 10

She went upstairs and found three beds. There was a great, big bed, a middle-sized bed, and a wee, little bed.

She lay on the big bed. "This one is too hard."
She lay on the middle-sized bed. "This one is too soft."
She lay on the small bed. "This one is just right." 12

And she fell fast asleep. 13

The three bears came home to eat their oatmeal.
"Someone has been eating my oatmeal,"
said Poppa in a great big voice.
"Someone has been eating my oatmeal," said
Momma in a middle-sized voice.

"Someone has been eating my oatmeal,"
said the baby bear, in a wee, little voice,
"and it's all gone!"

15

The three bears went into the living room.
"Someone has been sitting in my chair,"
said Poppa in a great big voice.
"Someone has been sitting in my chair,"
said Momma in a middle-sized voice.

"Someone has been sitting in my chair," said the
baby bear in a wee, little voice,
"and it's broken into pieces!" 17

The three bears went upstairs.
"Someone has been sleeping in my bed,"
said Poppa in a great big voice.
"Someone has been sleeping in my bed,"
said Momma in a middle-sized voice.

"Someone has been sleeping in my bed," said the baby bear in a wee, little voice, "and there she is!" 19

Goldilocks woke up and saw the three bears.

She ran away and never went back! —The End 21

Goldilocks and the Three Bears

Goldilocks and the Three Bears *(cont.)*

Goldilocks and the Three Bears *(cont.)*

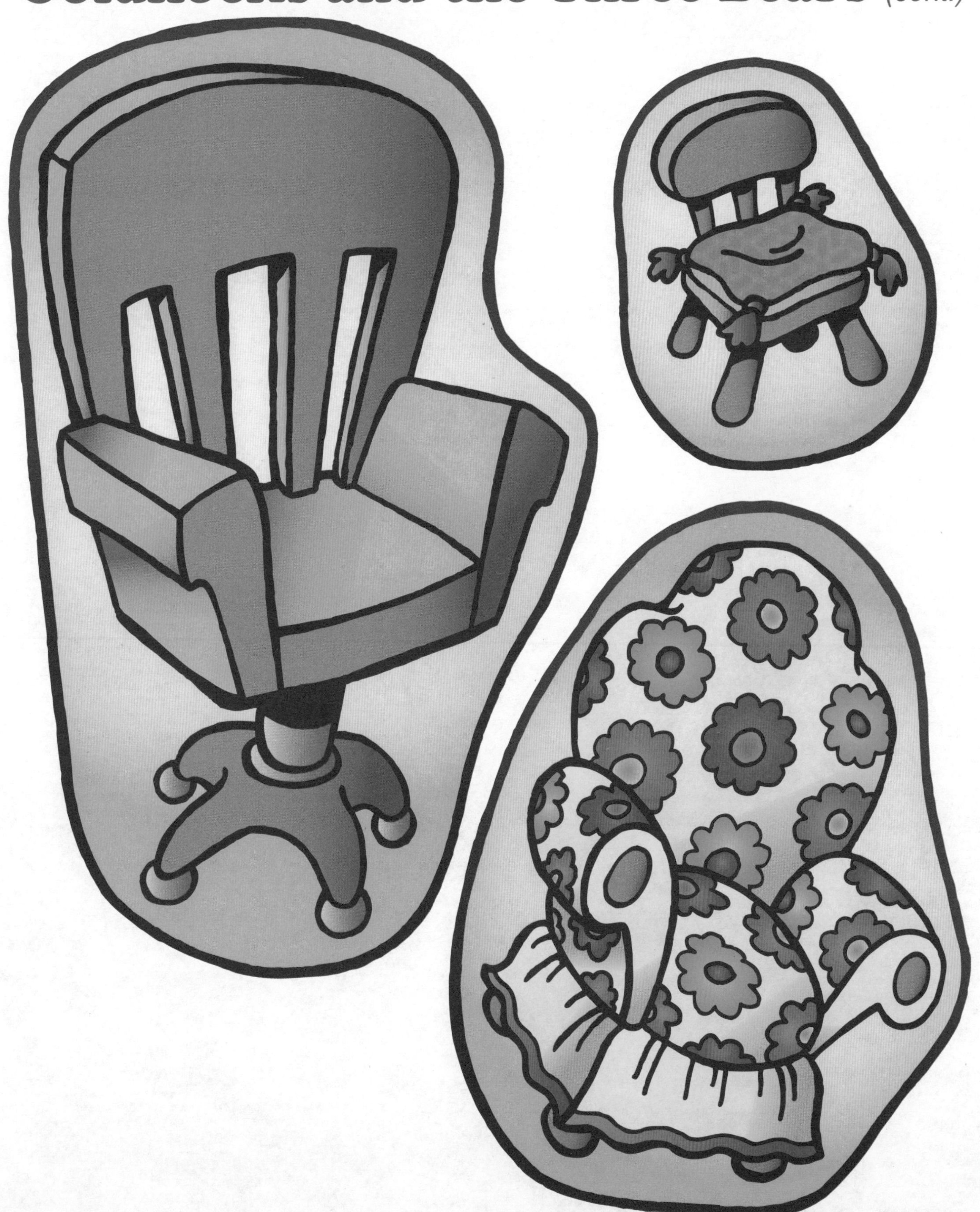

Goldilocks and the Three Bears *(cont.)*

The Three Billy Goats Gruff

Once upon a time there were three billy goat brothers named "Gruff."

Little Billy Goat Gruff was the youngest.

Middle Billy Goat Gruff was older.

Great Big Billy Goat Gruff was the oldest of them all.

The billy goats Gruff wanted to eat the sweet green grass on the other side of the river, but they had to cross a bridge with a mean, nasty troll underneath.

Little Billy Goat Gruff walked onto the bridge.

Trip, trap, trip, trap, went his little hooves on the bridge.

Up jumped the troll, and he roared, "Who's that trip-trapping over my bridge?"

"It is I, Little Billy Goat Gruff," answered the goat.

"I'm going to eat you up!" roared the troll.

"No, wait!" cried the Little Billy Goat Gruff.

"I am only a small billy goat. Wait for my brother—
he's much bigger than I am!"

"Very well then," growled the troll, *"be off with you!"*

And the Little Billy Goat Gruff trip-trapped across the bridge and went to eat the sweet green grass.

Middle Billy Goat Gruff went onto the bridge.

Trip, trap, trip, trap, went his middle-sized hooves on the bridge.

Up jumped the troll, and he roared, *"Who's that trip-trapping over my bridge?"*

"It is I, Middle Billy Goat Gruff," answered the goat.

"I'm going to eat you up!" roared the troll.

"No, wait!" cried the Middle Billy Goat Gruff.

"I am only a middle-sized billy goat. Wait for my brother—
he's much bigger than I am!"

"Very well then," growled the troll, *"be off with you!"*

And the Middle Billy Goat Gruff trip-trapped across the bridge and went to eat the sweet green grass.

Great Big Billy Goat Gruff went onto the bridge.

TRIP, TRAP, TRIP, TRAP, went his big hooves on the bridge.

Up jumped the troll, and he roared, *"Who's that trip-trapping over my bridge?"*

"It is I, Great Big Billy Goat Gruff," answered the goat.

"I'm going to eat you up!" roared the troll.

Great Big Billy Goat Gruff did not answer. He lowered his head and ran straight at the troll. He butted the troll off the bridge and into the water!

The troll floated away and was never seen again.

Great Big Billy Goat Gruff **TRIP-TRAPPED** over the bridge and ate the sweet, green grass with his brothers. — **The End**

The Three Billy Goats Gruff

Once upon a time there were three billy goat brothers named "Gruff."

1

Little Billy Goat Gruff was the youngest.
Middle Billy Goat Gruff was older.
Great Big Billy Goat Gruff was the oldest of them all.

The billy goats Gruff wanted to eat the sweet green grass on the other side of the river, but they had to cross a bridge with a mean, nasty troll underneath.

3

Little Billy Goat Gruff walked onto the bridge. *Trip, trap, trip, trap,* went his little hooves on the bridge.

4

Up jumped the troll, and he roared, "Who's that trip–trapping over my bridge?" "It is I, Little Billy Goat Gruff," answered the goat.

5

"I'm going to eat you up!" roared the troll. 

"No, wait!" cried the Little Billy Goat Gruff. "I am only a small billy goat. Wait for my brother—he's much bigger than I am!" 7

"Very well then," growled the troll,
"be off with you!"
And the Little Billy Goat Gruff *trip–trapped* across the bridge and went to eat the sweet green grass. 8

Middle Billy Goat Gruff went onto the bridge. *Trip, trap, trip, trap,* went his middle–sized hooves on the bridge. 9

Up jumped the troll, and he roared,
"Who's that trip–trapping over my bridge?"
"It is I, Middle Billy Goat Gruff,"
answered the goat.

10

"I'm going to eat you up!" roared the troll.

"No, wait!" cried the Middle Billy Goat Gruff. "I am only a middle-sized billy goat. Wait for my brother—he's much bigger than I am!" 12

"Very well then," growled the troll, "be off with you!"
And the Middle Billy Goat Gruff *trip-trapped* across the bridge and went to eat the sweet green grass. 13

Great Big Billy Goat Gruff went onto the bridge.
TRIP, TRAP, TRIP, TRAP,
went his big hooves on the bridge. 14

Up jumped the troll, and he roared,
"Who's that trip–trapping over my bridge?"
"It is I, Great Big Billy Goat Gruff,"
answered the goat. 15

"I'm going to eat you up!" roared the troll.

Great Big Billy Goat Gruff did not answer.
He lowered his head and ran straight at the troll.

He butted the troll off the bridge and into the water!
The troll floated away and was never seen again. 18

Great Big Billy Goat Gruff TRIP-TRAPPED over the bridge and ate the sweet, green grass with his brothers.

—The End 19

Name: ____________________

Three Billy Goats Gruff

Directions: Cut out the goats on the dotted lines. Glue the goats on the bridge in size order.

Billy Goat Puppets

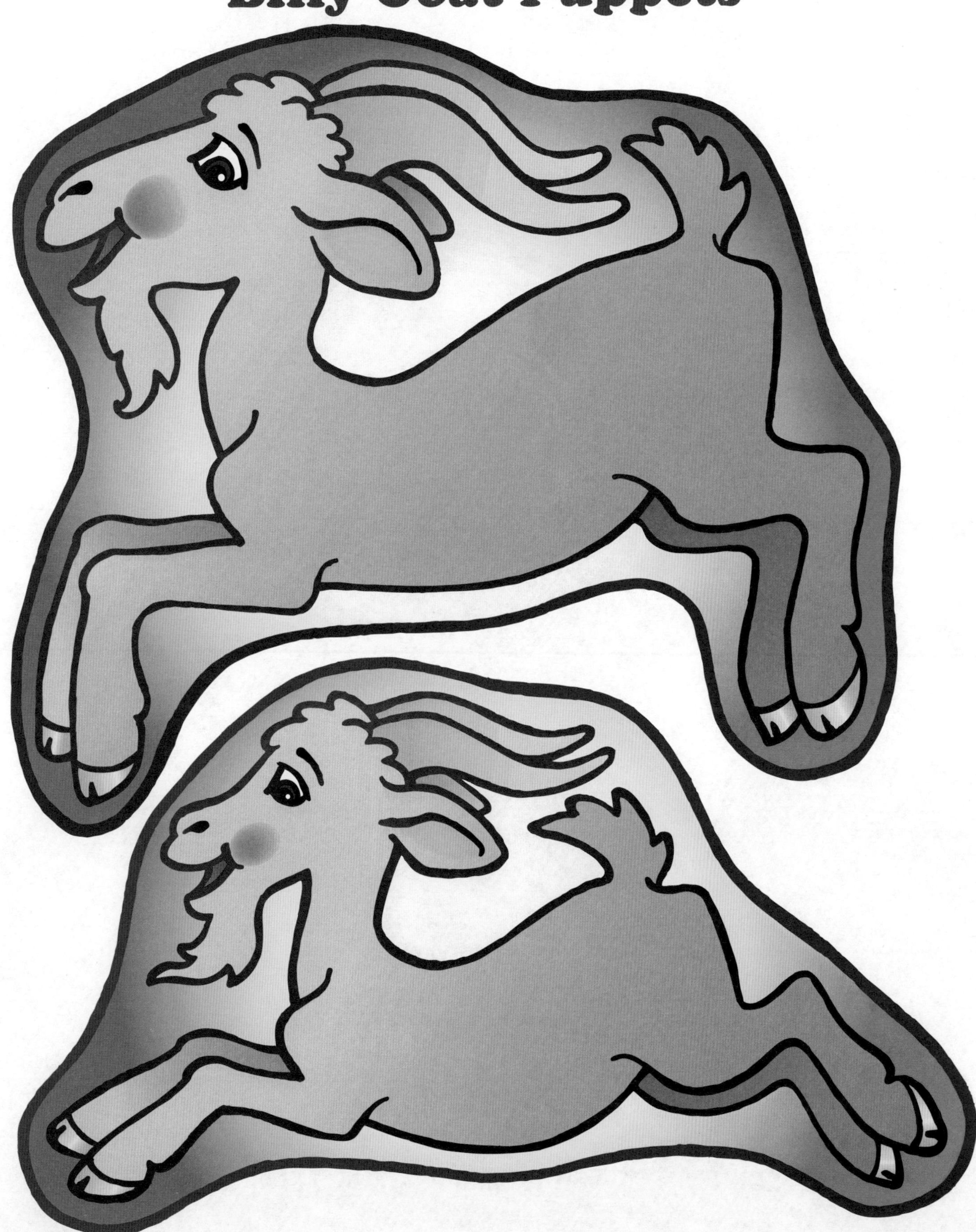

Billy Goat and Troll Puppets

Position & Location

Standard: *Understands the common language used to describe position and location*

Presentation Ideas

Jack Be Nimble

Cut out the candle on page 159 and laminate it. Read the first verse of "Jack Be Nimble" aloud to students, then have them repeat the rhyme with you. Place the cutout candlestick on the floor and ask a student (or students) to act out jumping over the candlestick. To make it more fun, you can change Jack to a student's name.

Read the second verse of the rhyme aloud to the class and have them repeat it with you. Hold the candlestick above students' heads and have them act out going under the candlestick.

Repeat this process with "jump on" and "stand in front of." Ask students to suggest other position words they could use in the rhyme ("jump off," "stand behind"). You can use any of these position words in the rhyme: over, under, below, above, beside, next to, on, off, in front, behind, left, right.

Copy the Jack, Jane, and candlestick (page 156) for each student. Tell students to choose either Jack or Jane, then color and cut out their choice of character and the candlestick. Give each student a large sheet of paper. Ask students to choose one position term and have them glue Jack or Jane and the candlestick onto the paper to illustrate the term. For example, a student who chooses "beside" should glue Jane beside the candlestick. Students can write or dictate a sentence such as "Jane is beside the candlestick." Collect the papers into a class book on positions.

The Grand Old Duke of York

Teach students "The Grand Old Duke of York" song (page 161). Have them act out the song by standing on the word "up" and squatting down on the word "down" in the first verse and stepping to the left or to the right in the second verse. This is great fun and a good way to reinforce the position words *up, down, left* and *right*.

Cut out and laminate the soldier puppets (page 163) and use it to act out the rhyme. Cut out the holes and put your fingers through to make the soldier's legs, then "walk" him up the hill, down the hill, and to the left and right. Before you cut out the puppet, you may want to make copies so you can make extra puppets for the students.

Jack, Jane, and Candlestick

Jack Be Nimble

Jack be nimble
Jack be quick
Jack jump *over* the candlestick.

Jack be nimble
Jack be quick
Jack go *under* the candlestick.

Jane be nimble
Jane be quick
Jane jump *on* the candlestick.

Jane be nimble
Jane be quick
Jane *stand in front* of the candlestick.

Jack Be Nimble

Jack be nimble
Jack be quick
Jack jump *over* the candlestick.

Jack be nimble
Jack be quick
Jack go *under* the candlestick.

Jane be nimble
Jane be quick
Jane jump *on* the candlestick.

Jane be nimble
Jane be quick
Jane *stand in front* of the candlestick.

Candlestick

The Grand Old Duke of York

The Grand Old Duke of York
He had ten thousand men.
He marched them *up* to the top of the hill
And marched them *down* again!

And when you're up you're up,
And when you're down you're down.
And when you're only halfway up,
You're neither up nor down.

The Grand Old Duke of York
He had ten thousand men.
He marched them to the *left* of the hill
And marched them *right* again.

And when you're left you're left,
And when you're right you're right,
And when you're smack in the middle then
You're neither left nor right.

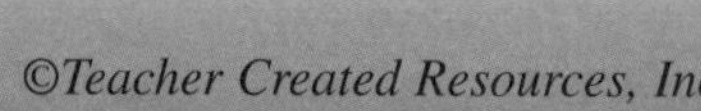

The Grand Old Duke of York

The Grand Old Duke of York
He had ten thousand men.
He marched them *up* to the top of the hill
And marched them *down* again!

And when you're up you're up,
And when you're down you're down.
And when you're only halfway up,
You're neither up nor down.

The Grand Old Duke of York
He had ten thousand men.
He marched them to the *left* of the hill
And marched them *right* again.

And when you're left you're left,
And when you're right you're right,
And when you're smack in the middle then
You're neither left nor right.

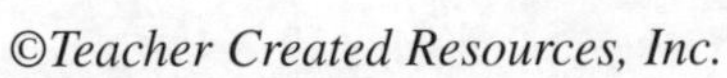

Soldier Puppets

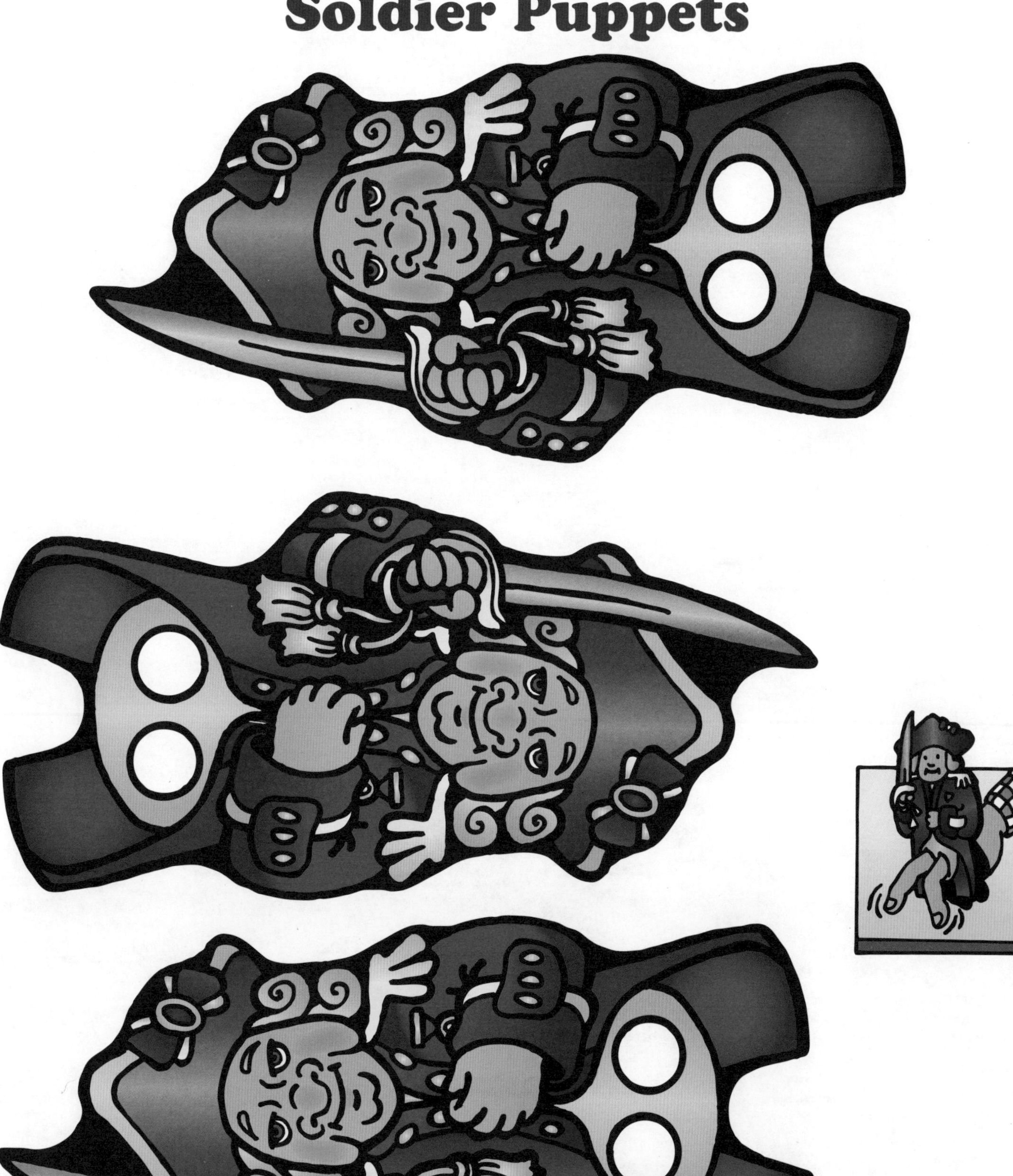

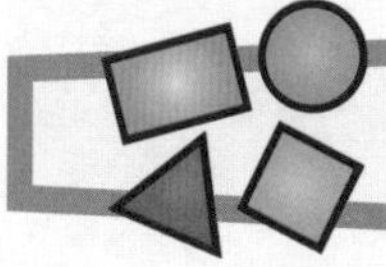

Shapes

Standards: *Knows basic geometric language for naming shapes (e.g., circle, triangle, square, rectangle)*
Understands basic properties of (e.g., number of sides, corners) and similarities and differences between simple geometric shapes

Presentation Ideas

- Cut out and laminate the color shapes on pages 171–173. Introduce each shape to students by reading "The Shape Poem" (page 167) and pointing out and counting the number of sides and corners on each shape. As you read the poem again, have students trace each shape in the air with a finger and say its name.
- Sing "The Shape Song" (page 169) for students. As you sing each verse, leave out the name of the shape ("I'm a …") and ask students to name the shape. Teach students the song and let them take turns singing a verse and asking the class to give the name of the shape.
- Copy the reproducible shapes on page 166 for each student. Have students color and cut out each shape. Teach students the "Where Is Triangle?" song (below). Sing a verse for each shape by replacing the word "triangle" with "square," "circle," or "rectangle." Have students hold up the appropriate shape for each verse. This activity can be used to assess students' knowledge of shapes.

Where is Triangle?

Where is triangle? Where is triangle?
Here I am. Here I am.
How are you today, sir? Very well, I thank you.
Run away. Run away.

(Try singing to the tune of "Where is Thumbkin?")

- Cut out and laminate the Shape Word Cards (page 175). Introduce each word to students, and place it in a pocket chart next to the correct shape. As students become more familiar with the shape names they can practice matching each shape to the correct word card.
- Use these songs and activities throughout the year to practice and reinforce shape identification.

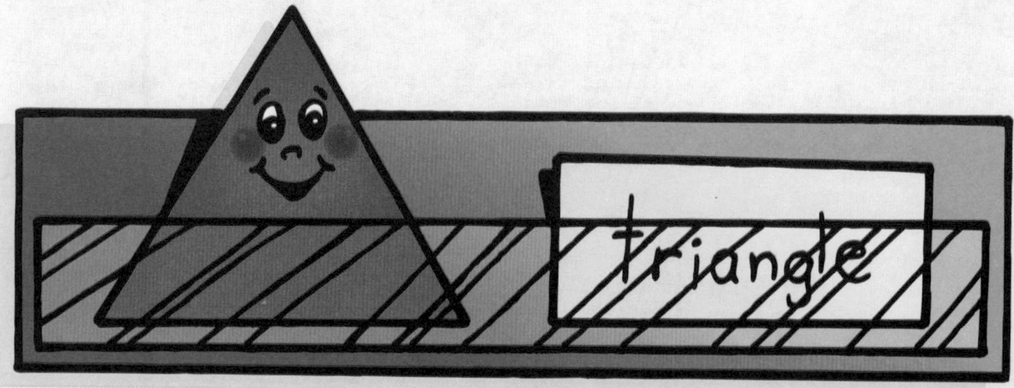

Reproducible Shapes

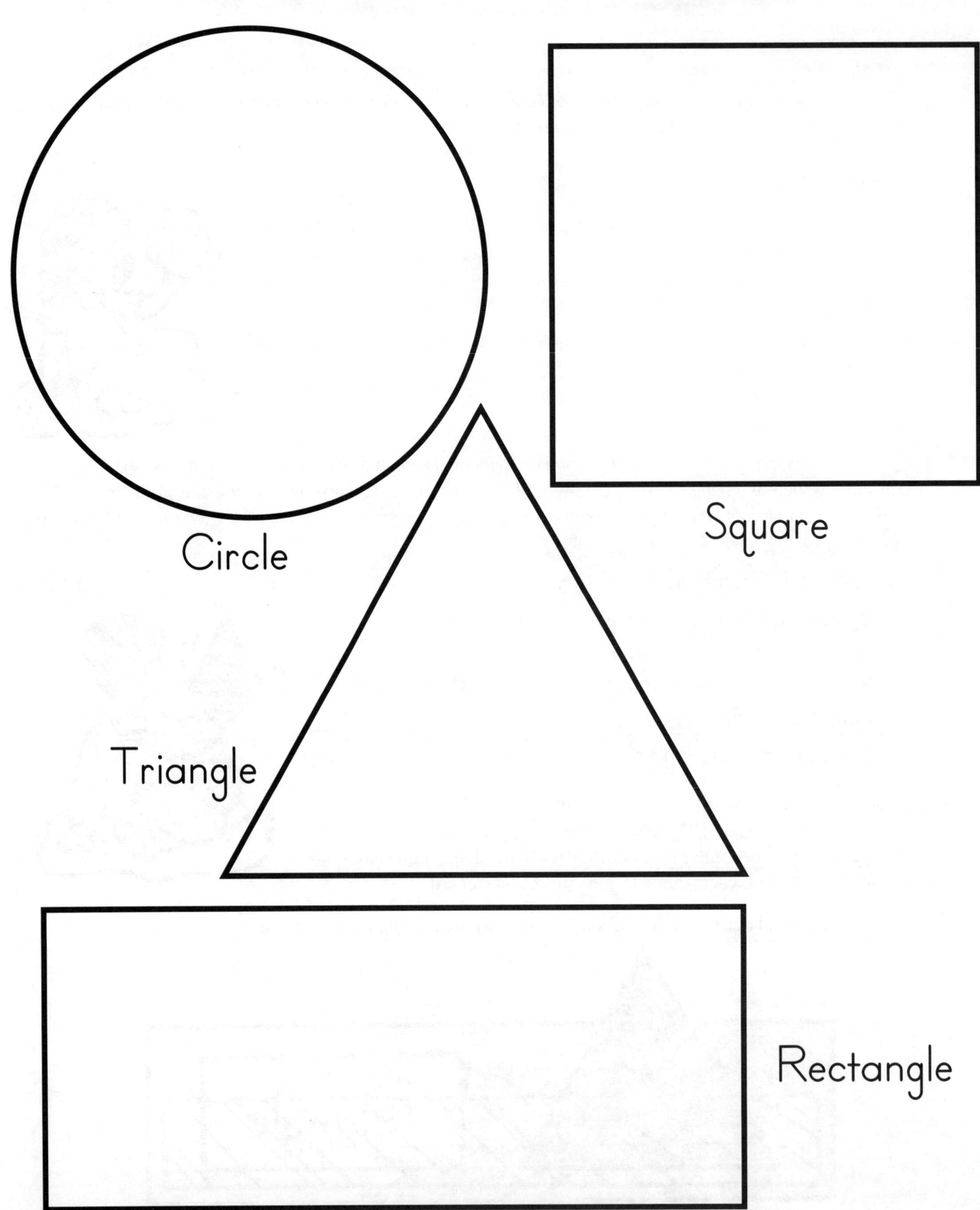

Shape Poem

I am a triangle,
three sides have I.

I am a circle,
round as a pie.

I am a square,
my sides are four.

I am a rectangle,
shaped like a door.

Shape Poem

I am a triangle,
three sides have I.

I am a circle,
round as a pie.

I am a square,
my sides are four.

I am a rectangle,
shaped like a door.

The Shape Song

(Try singing to the tune of "London Bridge")

Four straight sides are all the same
All the same, all the same
Four straight sides are all the same
I'm a *square*

Two sides short and two sides long
Two sides short, two sides long
Two sides short and two sides long
I'm a *rectangle*

Three sides, count them one, two, three
One, two, three; one, two, three
Three corners, count them one, two, three
I'm a *triangle*

I'm as round as I can be
I can be, I can be
I have no straight sides you see
I'm a *circle*

The Shape Song

(Try singing to the tune of "London Bridge")

Four straight sides are all the same
All the same, all the same
Four straight sides are all the same
I'm a *square*

Two sides short and two sides long
Two sides short, two sides long
Two sides short and two sides long
I'm a *rectangle*

Three sides, count them one, two, three
One, two, three; one, two, three
Three corners, count them one, two, three
I'm a *triangle*

I'm as round as I can be
I can be, I can be
I have no straight sides you see
I'm a *circle*

Circle

Triangle

Square

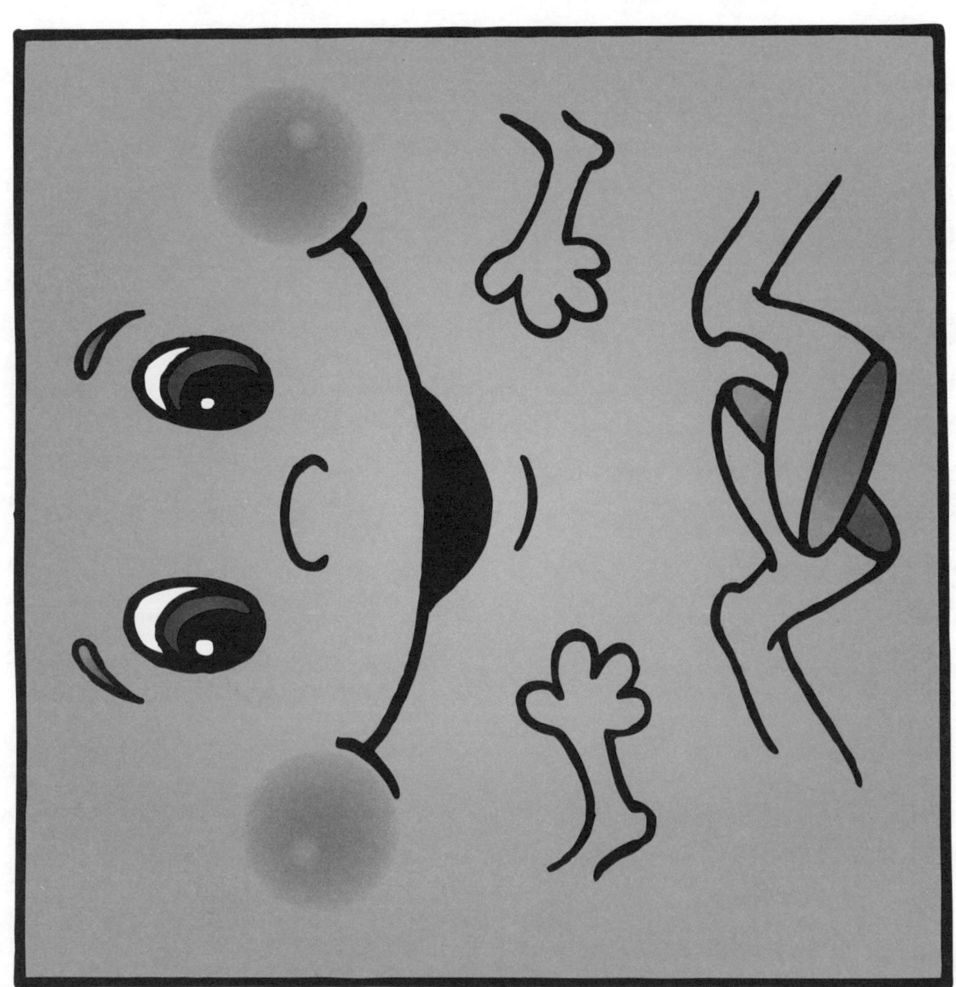

Rectangle

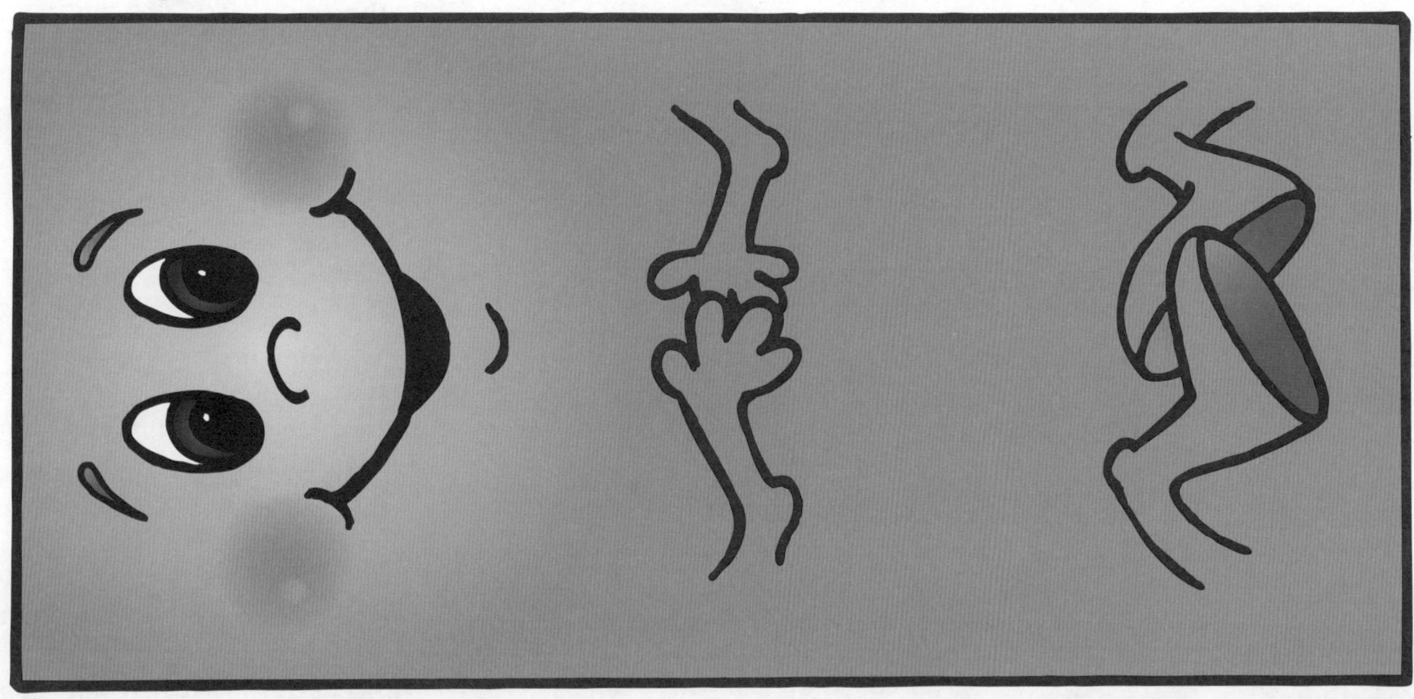

square

circle

rectangle

triangle

Teacher
Created
Resources